COASTAL GARDENING *in the* PACIFIC NORTHWEST

COASTAL GARDENING *in the*

PACIFIC NORTHWEST

*From Northern California to
British Columbia*

CARLA ALBRIGHT

Taylor Trade Publishing
Lanham • Boulder • New York • Toronto • Plymouth, UK

This Taylor Trade Publishing paperback edition of *Coastal Gardening in the Pacific Northwest* is an original publication. It is published by arrangement with the author.

Published by Taylor Trade Publishing

An imprint of The Rowman & Littlefield Publishing Group, Inc.

4501 Forbes Boulevard, Suite 200, Lanham, Maryland 20706

Distributed by NATIONAL BOOK NETWORK

Library of Congress Cataloging-in-Publication Data

Albright, Carla.

Coastal gardening in the Pacific Northwest : from Northern California to British Columbia / Carla Albright. — 1st Taylor Trade Publishing ed.

p. cm.

ISBN-13: 978-1-58979-317-0 (paper)

1. Seaside gardening—Northwest, Pacific. 2. Coastal plants—Northwest, Pacific. 3. Seaside gardening—California, Northern. 4. Coastal plants—California, Northern. I. Title.

SB460.A43 2007

635.9'51795—dc22

2006032030

To:
Gary, Gene, and Rebecca,
Hobart, Levee, Mandy, Joanne and Gert.
My family, two- and four-legged.

CONTENTS

I WOULD BE REMISS if I did not start by thanking my dear mother for teaching me the difference between a weed and a portulaca. And how wonderful it is to eat a tomato out of the garden. Working beside her in her little rock garden are some of my fondest memories of growing up. Now in my own garden, I often ask myself, "What would my mother have done here?" Gone too soon, I still miss her every day.

My gardening friends over the years have also inspired me. Betty, the British gardener, Marlene, the German gardener, and Dena, the American one, have all contributed to my love of gardening in ways they probably don't realize. Not to mention the Tillamook County master gardeners Sheila, Cris, Sally, Patty, Betsy, Evelynn, Janet, Jane, Mary, and Deborah, as well as all the others who have in their own ways encouraged me to write this book. Some were also generous enough to allow me to photograph their gardens and give me ideas to include. I thank you, ladies, all.

I also send a large thank you to Maggie MacLaren, professional garden photographer—and dear friend—who has given me permission to use one of her photographs on the cover. Maggie is one of those gardeners who are relatively new to the concept of a coastal garden, having relocated recently to Vancouver Island. Her generosity overwhelms me.

To my editor, Dulcie Wilcox, I owe a tremendous debt of gratitude. Dulcie saw potential in this book and encouraged me to run with it. For her countless hours of support—and editing—I thank her.

And lastly, but most importantly, I would like to thank my family: My dear husband of 36 years, Gary, who has always been my biggest fan and who first saw my writing capabilities and encouraged me to think about writing a book. And thank you to my son, Eugene, and our daughter-in-love, his dear wife, Rebecca, as they add such joy, encouragement, and humor to my life. I would not have attempted such a daunting task had I not had all of their love and support. The words have not yet been created that will fully express my love and gratitude to you all.

WHEN I MOVED to the north Oregon coast a few years ago, I was an experienced Zone 5 gardener. I was used to snowy, often frigid winters and hot, humid summers. My garden included mostly roses, herbs, perennials, and a few annuals. It was a good gardening climate but a short one. The days were hot enough and the summer long enough that the vegetable patch included tomatoes, corn, and, of course, the omnipresent zucchini.

But our son relocated to the Portland area—far away from western Pennsylvania where I had lived most of my life. Time for a change. Time to move to the coast.

Imagine my thrill to learn I was now living in a Zone 8. So many more plants and a much longer growing season. I went from gardening from May through September to gardening from late February through October and, in a good year, into November. But that longer growing season also came with strong winds, sandy soil, and salt spray. I needed some help to learn what I could—and couldn't—successfully grow here.

Enter the Master Gardener program. I had been a master gardener in the east through the Penn State University Extension Service and had chosen an Oregon county to live in that also had a Master Gardener program, this time through Oregon State University Extension Service. I took the training classes the first winter here, knowing I would learn specifics about coastal gardening. And I did.

In the following chapters, you will hear me refer to "your local extension office" quite often. Perhaps a bit of background is in order. In the United States, each individual state has what is called a "land-grant" college. These are generally the agriculture schools for the states, and are usually called "Penn State," "Oregon State," "Washington State," and so on. Each of these land-grant colleges maintain county extension offices that address questions and concerns from the agricultural community. The 4-H program is one of the extensions' most visible projects. In the late 1970s, Washington State University's extension offices were finding themselves inundated with questions from home gardeners. One of their extension agents came up with the idea of training volunteers to answer those questions so that the agent could be available for the local commercial farmers instead of the local hobby gardeners. Thus began the Master Gardener training program. There are now master gardeners in every state nationwide and in the Canadian provinces as well. All master gardeners go through an extensive training program for home horticulture in exchange for donating hours of service to their respective communities. This was the training I underwent in both Pennsylvania and Oregon.

I also needed some supplemental help with specifics and looked for books on Pacific Northwest coastal gardening. I found a few plant lists and a great book on native plants, but not much else. The books for coastal North and South Carolina weren't relevant to the cool damp climate we have here. When I found other gardeners new to the area also expressing frustration in finding localized information, I thought I should compile what I had learned as a master gardener with the additional information I had culled from various sources for my own use. I added photographs I had taken from my own gardens as well as those of my friends, and before I realized it, I had written a book on coastal gardening for the Pacific Northwest.

You will notice that I use botanical names as well as common names. Botanical nomenclature is becoming more common for the straightforward reason that we need to know precisely what plant we are discussing. The term "dusty miller," for example, can mean one of seven or eight different plants. Try to become familiar with botanical names to avoid confusion, especially when shopping for plants.

I have learned even more about coastal gardening as I have done the research for this book. Hopefully it will aid the beginning gardener as well as the experienced inland gardener who has relocated to the coastal areas.

The range of styles discussed varies from the simple lines of the Japanese Zen garden to the "blowsy" look of the English cottage garden and a few designs in between. I have visited the gardens I have written about and hope the reader will take the time to do so as well. Some of the gardens that I have photographed are private and unavailable for study by the general community, but I have also listed many public gardens that gardeners from all levels of experience can learn from and enjoy.

And that's what gardening should be: a learning experience but also an enjoyable one.

COASTAL GARDENING *in the* PACIFIC NORTHWEST

ONE

THE BASICS

THE BEAUTY AND UNIQUENESS of the Pacific Northwest coast can also be the reasons coastal gardening may be so difficult. The ocean meets the mountains in many places and in between there are miles of sand dunes, beach grass, and scrub pines.

A person coming to this area for the first time will be struck by its beauty. The winds and the salt water will be refreshing and invigorating.

A gardener moving to this area for the first time will be struck by its harshness and difficult growing conditions. The gardener will find the wind and salt water to be challenging and demanding.

An informed gardener who takes time to explore this coastal area will, however, find many gardens—both private and public—of beauty and interest.

Novice and experienced gardeners alike can take solace in the mild winter and the moderate summer temperatures, both of which extend the growing season for many plants.

Geography is important even though it isn't taught in many schools anymore. The proximity to the ocean can have a drastic effect on what can easily be grown. Proximity to the mountains will also have an effect, as does the corresponding elevation. There are work pages throughout this chapter for you to record information such as site maps and temperatures. This book can also act as a garden journal. Included in it are questions to ask and answer yourself that will guide you when designing your garden.

Whether you are new to gardening or new to coastal gardening, you can have a beautiful, easily maintained garden by following these steps.

But try, if you can, to be patient. This may be difficult. We gardeners are not patient by nature. Most of the time we want instant gratification; we want lots of flowers and we want them now! If this is your nature, too, that's normal, but may I suggest the first summer you are gardening on the coast you purchase annuals for that instant color? Don't spend a lot of money or time on expensive perennials and shrubs and trees until you better know your garden. This may take up to a year, so again I advise, "Be patient!"

A good garden, one you can enjoy for many years, takes time to plan, plant, and evolve.

STEP ONE: ASSESSING THE CONDITIONS IN YOUR GARDEN OR GARDEN-TO-BE

Here are some questions you need to ask yourself before you begin. Jot the answers down as you work through the book to serve as a reference when you begin your design plan.

1. Can I see the ocean from my yard? _____Do I live within five miles of the ocean? _____
   This will affect soil type, wind, and sun. It may also increase or decrease your USDA zone and thus your plant choices.

2. What is my approximate elevation? _____How far above sea level is my garden? _____
   Elevation will affect the temperature of your garden's soil in the spring. It will also have an effect on the amount and form of precipitation you receive.

3. Is there a slope to my yard? _____Toward which direction? _____Is it enough of a grade to affect sunlight and erosion? _____Will rain run-off be a problem? _____
   Slope may be something you can live with or something that needs to be corrected. How much correction the slope needs will depend on the type of garden you wish to have.

4. What blocks my sunlight? _____
   _____
   This can be a house, garage, shed, a tree, a neighbor's house, a neighbor's tree, or even a mountain. List everything you see around you. This list may change with the seasons. Sun movement, deciduous trees, and wind direction are all variables.

5. Do I live in the woods? _____By a sand dune? _____In a town or a village? _____
   The location of your house will often times reflect the type, size, and location of your garden.

6. What kind of a garden do I want to have? _____
   Do I want vegetables or flowers or both? _____
   Do I want evergreen trees and shrubs or deciduous ones that will lose their leaves each fall? _____ Are there different areas I can use for different purposes? _____
   No need to worry about the focus or design at this stage. That will come later. We just need to be thinking about a general use of the garden.
7. Do I get a lot of wind? _____ When and from which direction does it come? _____ Is it blocked by anything? _____
   (Fences, buildings, trees, etc.)
   Winds, as we mentioned in Question 4, also change course from summer to winter. Make a note of the general direction each season.
   Winter: _____
   Spring: _____
   Summer: _____
   Fall: _____.
   Most windy gardens will benefit from a windbreak of some type, so be thinking of what you prefer: something growing like a hedge or shrubs or something man-made like a fence.
   Do you like a natural feel or one that is more modern and industrial? _____
8. How cold does it get in the winter? _____ How hot does it get in the summer? _____ How much rainfall do I get each year? _____ Do I ever get snow or ice storms? _____
   These questions are important when you start to plan the types of plants that will do well. We are aiming for success and not frustration.
9. What is my USDA Zone? _____
   To identify your zone, you need a USDA Plant Hardiness Map. See Step Two.

STEP TWO: CLIMATES AND MICROCLIMATES

Once you have answered the questions in Step One, you need to find out your climate zone. We will use the USDA and AHS maps to determine your zone.

USDA and AHS Zones

The United States Department of Agriculture periodically issues a "USDA Plant Hardiness Map." The most recent was issued in March of 2003. These maps have the country broken down into colored areas according to their average annual minimum temperatures in a winter. For example, the USDA map shows southern coastal Oregon and parts of southern coastal Washington in a Zone 9. This means the average minimum winter temperatures are between 30 to 20 degrees. Northern coastal Oregon is in a Zone 8. These average annual minimum temperatures are between 20 and 10 degrees. (Many people along the coast will contest these figures because of mild winters, but these temperatures are what the USDA bases their maps upon.) To clarify a little further, the higher the zonal number, the warmer the winters tend to be. In a plant catalog, if a plant is listed as "Zone 5–8," for example, it would do well in Ohio's harsher winters, but also in Oregon coastal winters. The winters in southern Oregon's Zone 9, however, may be too warm.

To further interpret things a bit, in 1997, the American Horticultural Society issued a heat-tolerance map, showing areas of similar summer temperatures. On this "Plant Heat-Zone Map," most of coastal Oregon and Washington are Zone 2. This means the number of days in a summer that the temperature rises above 85 degrees (Fahrenheit) is one to seven in an average year.

Gardening magazines and catalogs will have a current Plant Hardiness map located somewhere within their pages. Some now also include a Heat-Tolerance map as well, and list plants, for example, by "Hardiness Zones 5 to 8 / Heat Zones from 1 to 2." By using these maps and knowing your zone, you can more easily choose plants that will do well in your geographical area.

One of the easiest divisions of zones I have seen is by Ray and Jan McNeilan in their *Pacific Northwest Gardener's Book of Lists*, published in 1997. They simplify things for us by using the terms Coastal, Low Mountains, Low Valleys, Dry Valleys, and High Desert. For our purposes, we will be dealing with the "Coastal Areas" (USDA Zones 8 and 9), which is defined by areas on the Oregon and Washington coasts or an area that is influenced by the coastal climate, soils, and rainfall. We will also be talking about "Low Mountain Areas," which have a mild, medium-length growing season but may have some snow for brief periods in the winter (USDA Zone 7). This mostly describes areas west of the coastal mountain ranges from the Canadian border to northern California.

Now that you know your climate zone, you can start to break down your yard into "microclimates." This sounds harder than it really is. A microclimate is simply a small area where the climate is different from the majority of your yard and the yards around you. It can be colder or warmer and it can get more or less precipitation, be it in the form of rain—like most of the coast—or as snow in higher elevations. Most yards have areas that get more sun or more wind than other areas. Rainfall generally is the same except under porches, eaves and other forms of shelter. You will know what areas seem to be colder in the winter and warmer in the summer if you pay attention. And because each part of your garden has its own special little conditions, its own microclimate, you will be able to grow different plants in those specialized areas.

Start by sketching a map on the following pages of the different areas of your garden. There are graphed pages to make it easier for you, and you can use a pencil for ease of changing later. The pages are laid out so that you can add data after each map. Find the compass rose in the corner and use it to indicate which direction is north. We aren't so much worried about structures here except where they will affect your sunlight or block the wind, so place them along the edges of the map. The maps are to be of your garden's areas, not your whole lot. Try to keep your map as much in scale as possible. Be sure to include all current plants that are either too large to move or that you want to keep in the garden, and mark them by name if you can, estimating their height and width. Your map doesn't have to be elaborate or fancy because it's not going on display. Use a separate map page for each area.

Now when you stroll through your yard throughout the year, take this workbook, a pencil and a small thermometer. Jot down the date, the time, the location of the sun, and the temperature. Track the line of the sun as it moves from east to west, noting which areas of your garden are affected and how. Be sure to note if there is any wind when you are out and from which direction it is coming. Judge how harsh the wind is: breeze, light, medium, strong, or gale force? Is it raining? If so, how hard? Vary the times of day when you visit the area, and note any observations. This is not an exact science, but if you do each area on a bimonthly basis, you can start to see patterns of the microclimates. This will help in your choice of plants. You can see which areas are sunny and dry, sunny and wet, dry shade, or damp shade. Take photographs of your garden areas from inside the house as well as outside. This will be an additional help in planning since you will want your garden to look as good from the inside of your home as it does from the outside.

The type of garden you create will depend upon the size and shape of the area to be covered as well as the major elements you choose to incorporate. Before you start laying out the plans, and certainly before you start digging, be sure to call the local utility hotline to locate any underground wires or pipes. They will come out and mark the lines for you with flags or spray paint. Once the utilities are marked, you will have a better idea of where you can successfully plant without disturbing those lines. Put these lines on your site map before you begin laying out your designs on paper.

Area One: _____

Place your buildings and out structures along the edges, leaving the graph area for yard shape and size. One inch = one foot.

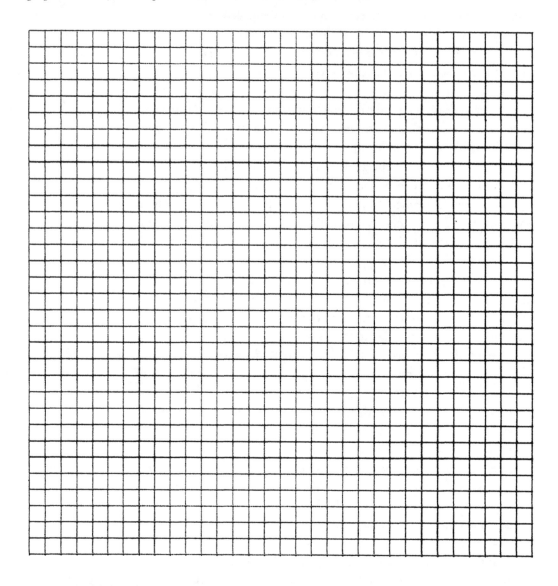

January 1:
Rainfall _____ Sunny ❑ Overcast ❑
Wind Speed _____ Wind Direction _____
High Temperature _____ Low Temperature _____
Plants in Bloom: _____
Other Notes:_____
_____

January 15:
Rainfall _____ Sunny ❑ Overcast ❑
Wind Speed _____ Wind Direction _____
High Temperature _____ Low Temperature _____
Plants in Bloom: _____
Other Notes:_____
_____

February 1:
Rainfall _____ Sunny ❑ Overcast ❑
Wind Speed _____ Wind Direction _____
High Temperature _____ Low Temperature _____
Plants in Bloom: _____
Other Notes:_____
_____

February 15:
Rainfall _____ Sunny ❑ Overcast ❑
Wind Speed _____ Wind Direction _____
High Temperature _____ Low Temperature _____
Plants in Bloom: _____
Other Notes:_____
_____

March 1:
Rainfall _____ Sunny ❑ Overcast ❑
Wind Speed _____ Wind Direction _____
High Temperature _____ Low Temperature _____
Plants in Bloom: _____
Other Notes:_____
_____

March 15:

Rainfall _____ Sunny ❏ Overcast ❏

Wind Speed _____ Wind Direction _____

High Temperature _____ Low Temperature _____

Plants in Bloom: _____

Other Notes:_____

_____

April 1:

Rainfall _____ Sunny ❏ Overcast ❏

Wind Speed _____ Wind Direction _____

High Temperature _____ Low Temperature _____

Plants in Bloom: _____

Other Notes:_____

_____

April 15:

Rainfall _____ Sunny ❏ Overcast ❏

Wind Speed _____ Wind Direction _____

High Temperature _____ Low Temperature _____

Plants in Bloom: _____

Other Notes:_____

_____

May 1:

Rainfall _____ Sunny ❏ Overcast ❏

Wind Speed _____ Wind Direction _____

High Temperature _____ Low Temperature _____

Plants in Bloom: _____

Other Notes:_____

_____

May 15:

Rainfall _____ Sunny ❏ Overcast ❏

Wind Speed _____ Wind Direction _____

High Temperature _____ Low Temperature _____

Plants in Bloom: _____

Other Notes:_____

_____

June 1:
Rainfall _____ Sunny ❑ Overcast ❑
Wind Speed _____ Wind Direction _____
High Temperature _____ Low Temperature _____
Plants in Bloom: _____
Other Notes:_____
_____

June 15:
Rainfall _____ Sunny ❑ Overcast ❑
Wind Speed _____ Wind Direction _____
High Temperature _____ Low Temperature _____
Plants in Bloom: _____
Other Notes:_____
_____

July 1:
Rainfall _____ Sunny ❑ Overcast ❑
Wind Speed _____ Wind Direction _____
High Temperature _____ Low Temperature _____
Plants in Bloom: _____
Other Notes:_____
_____

July 15:
Rainfall _____ Sunny ❑ Overcast ❑
Wind Speed _____ Wind Direction _____
High Temperature _____ Low Temperature _____
Plants in Bloom: _____
Other Notes:_____
_____

August 1:
Rainfall _____ Sunny ❑ Overcast ❑
Wind Speed _____ Wind Direction _____
High Temperature _____ Low Temperature _____
Plants in Bloom: _____
Other Notes:_____
_____

August 15:
Rainfall _____ Sunny ❑ Overcast ❑
Wind Speed _____ Wind Direction _____
High Temperature _____ Low Temperature _____
Plants in Bloom: _____
Other Notes:_____
_____

September 1:
Rainfall _____ Sunny ❑ Overcast ❑
Wind Speed _____ Wind Direction _____
High Temperature _____ Low Temperature _____
Plants in Bloom: _____
Other Notes:_____
_____

September 15:
Rainfall _____ Sunny ❑ Overcast ❑
Wind Speed _____ Wind Direction _____
High Temperature _____ Low Temperature _____
Plants in Bloom: _____
Other Notes:_____
_____

October 1:
Rainfall _____ Sunny ❑ Overcast ❑
Wind Speed _____ Wind Direction _____
High Temperature _____ Low Temperature _____
Plants in Bloom: _____
Other Notes:_____
_____

October 15:
Rainfall _____ Sunny ❑ Overcast ❑
Wind Speed _____ Wind Direction _____
High Temperature _____ Low Temperature _____
Plants in Bloom: _____
Other Notes:_____
_____

November 1:
Rainfall _____ Sunny ❑ Overcast ❑
Wind Speed _____ Wind Direction _____
High Temperature _____ Low Temperature _____
Plants in Bloom: _____
Other Notes:_____

_____

November 15:
Rainfall _____ Sunny ❑ Overcast ❑
Wind Speed _____ Wind Direction _____
High Temperature _____ Low Temperature _____
Plants in Bloom: _____
Other Notes:_____

_____

December 1:
Rainfall _____ Sunny ❑ Overcast ❑
Wind Speed _____ Wind Direction _____
High Temperature _____ Low Temperature _____
Plants in Bloom: _____
Other Notes:_____

_____

December 15:
Rainfall _____ Sunny ❑ Overcast ❑
Wind Speed _____ Wind Direction _____
High Temperature _____ Low Temperature _____
Plants in Bloom: _____
Other Notes:_____

_____

AREA ONE TOTALS
Rainfall _____
Date of Most Rainfall _____

Days of Sun _____
Days of Rain _____

Highest Temperature _____
Date of Highest Temperature _____

Lowest Temperature _____
Date of Lowest Temperature _____

Other Notes:_____

_____

Area Two: _____

Place your buildings and out structures along the edges, leaving the graph area for yard shape and size. One inch = one foot.

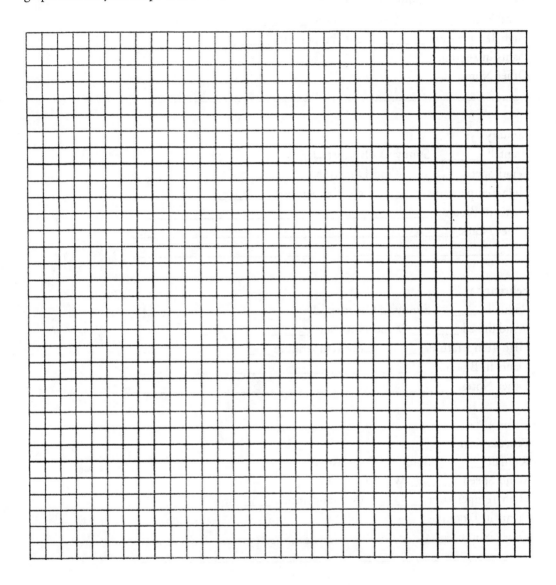

January 1:
Rainfall _____ Sunny ❑ Overcast ❑
Wind Speed _____ Wind Direction _____
High Temperature _____ Low Temperature _____
Plants in Bloom: _____
Other Notes:_____
_____

January 15:
Rainfall _____ Sunny ❑ Overcast ❑
Wind Speed _____ Wind Direction _____
High Temperature _____ Low Temperature _____
Plants in Bloom: _____
Other Notes:_____
_____

February 1:
Rainfall _____ Sunny ❑ Overcast ❑
Wind Speed _____ Wind Direction _____
High Temperature _____ Low Temperature _____
Plants in Bloom: _____
Other Notes:_____
_____

February 15:
Rainfall _____ Sunny ❑ Overcast ❑
Wind Speed _____ Wind Direction _____
High Temperature _____ Low Temperature _____
Plants in Bloom: _____
Other Notes:_____
_____

March 1:
Rainfall _____ Sunny ❑ Overcast ❑
Wind Speed _____ Wind Direction _____
High Temperature _____ Low Temperature _____
Plants in Bloom: _____
Other Notes:_____
_____

March 15:
Rainfall _____ Sunny ❑ Overcast ❑
Wind Speed _____ Wind Direction _____
High Temperature _____ Low Temperature _____
Plants in Bloom: _____
Other Notes:_____

_____

April 1:
Rainfall _____ Sunny ❑ Overcast ❑
Wind Speed _____ Wind Direction _____
High Temperature _____ Low Temperature _____
Plants in Bloom: _____
Other Notes:_____

_____

April 15:
Rainfall _____ Sunny ❑ Overcast ❑
Wind Speed _____ Wind Direction _____
High Temperature _____ Low Temperature _____
Plants in Bloom: _____
Other Notes:_____

_____

May 1:
Rainfall _____ Sunny ❑ Overcast ❑
Wind Speed _____ Wind Direction _____
High Temperature _____ Low Temperature _____
Plants in Bloom: _____
Other Notes:_____

_____

May 15:
Rainfall _____ Sunny ❑ Overcast ❑
Wind Speed _____ Wind Direction _____
High Temperature _____ Low Temperature _____
Plants in Bloom: _____
Other Notes:_____

_____

June 1:
Rainfall _____ Sunny ❏ Overcast ❏
Wind Speed _____ Wind Direction _____
High Temperature _____ Low Temperature _____
Plants in Bloom: _____
Other Notes:_____
_____

June 15:
Rainfall _____ Sunny ❏ Overcast ❏
Wind Speed _____ Wind Direction _____
High Temperature _____ Low Temperature _____
Plants in Bloom: _____
Other Notes:_____
_____

July 1:
Rainfall _____ Sunny ❏ Overcast ❏
Wind Speed _____ Wind Direction _____
High Temperature _____ Low Temperature _____
Plants in Bloom: _____
Other Notes:_____
_____

July 15:
Rainfall _____ Sunny ❏ Overcast ❏
Wind Speed _____ Wind Direction _____
High Temperature _____ Low Temperature _____
Plants in Bloom: _____
Other Notes:_____
_____

August 1:
Rainfall _____ Sunny ❏ Overcast ❏
Wind Speed _____ Wind Direction _____
High Temperature _____ Low Temperature _____
Plants in Bloom: _____
Other Notes:_____
_____

August 15:
Rainfall _____ Sunny ❑ Overcast ❑
Wind Speed _____ Wind Direction _____
High Temperature _____ Low Temperature _____
Plants in Bloom: _____
Other Notes:_____
_____

September 1:
Rainfall _____ Sunny ❑ Overcast ❑
Wind Speed _____ Wind Direction _____
High Temperature _____ Low Temperature _____
Plants in Bloom: _____
Other Notes:_____
_____

September 15:
Rainfall _____ Sunny ❑ Overcast ❑
Wind Speed _____ Wind Direction _____
High Temperature _____ Low Temperature _____
Plants in Bloom: _____
Other Notes:_____
_____

October 1:
Rainfall _____ Sunny ❑ Overcast ❑
Wind Speed _____ Wind Direction _____
High Temperature _____ Low Temperature _____
Plants in Bloom: _____
Other Notes:_____
_____

October 15:
Rainfall _____ Sunny ❑ Overcast ❑
Wind Speed _____ Wind Direction _____
High Temperature _____ Low Temperature _____
Plants in Bloom: _____
Other Notes:_____
_____

November 1:
Rainfall _____ Sunny ❑ Overcast ❑
Wind Speed _____ Wind Direction _____
High Temperature _____ Low Temperature _____
Plants in Bloom: _____
Other Notes:_____

_____

November 15:
Rainfall _____ Sunny ❑ Overcast ❑
Wind Speed _____ Wind Direction _____
High Temperature _____ Low Temperature _____
Plants in Bloom: _____
Other Notes:_____

_____

December 1:
Rainfall _____ Sunny ❑ Overcast ❑
Wind Speed _____ Wind Direction _____
High Temperature _____ Low Temperature _____
Plants in Bloom: _____
Other Notes:_____

_____

December 15:
Rainfall _____ Sunny ❑ Overcast ❑
Wind Speed _____ Wind Direction _____
High Temperature _____ Low Temperature _____
Plants in Bloom: _____
Other Notes:_____

_____

Coastal Gardening in the Pacific Northwest

AREA TWO TOTALS

Rainfall _____
Date of Most Rainfall _____

Days of Sun _____
Days of Rain _____

Highest Temperature _____
Date of Highest Temperature _____

Lowest Temperature _____
Date of Lowest Temperature _____

Other Notes:_____
_____

Area Three: _____

Place your buildings and out structures along the edges, leaving the graph area for yard shape and size. One inch = one foot

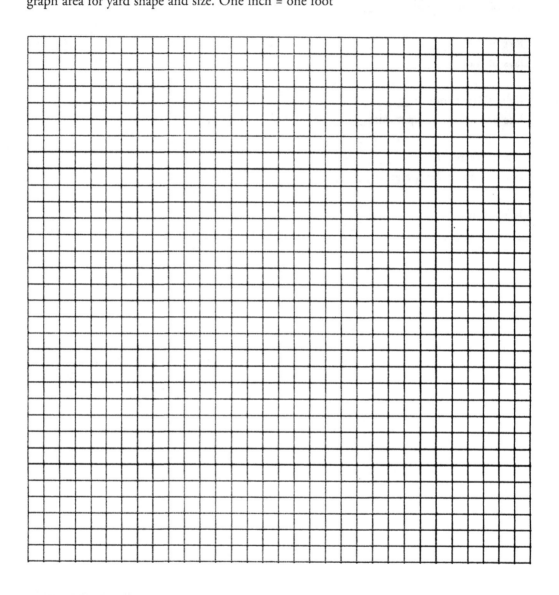

January 1:
Rainfall _____ Sunny ❑ Overcast ❑
Wind Speed _____ Wind Direction _____
High Temperature _____ Low Temperature _____
Plants in Bloom: _____
Other Notes:_____
_____

January 15:
Rainfall _____ Sunny ❑ Overcast ❑
Wind Speed _____ Wind Direction _____
High Temperature _____ Low Temperature _____
Plants in Bloom: _____
Other Notes:_____
_____

February 1:
Rainfall _____ Sunny ❑ Overcast ❑
Wind Speed _____ Wind Direction _____
High Temperature _____ Low Temperature _____
Plants in Bloom: _____
Other Notes:_____
_____

February 15:
Rainfall _____ Sunny ❑ Overcast ❑
Wind Speed _____ Wind Direction _____
High Temperature _____ Low Temperature _____
Plants in Bloom: _____
Other Notes:_____
_____

March 1:
Rainfall _____ Sunny ❑ Overcast ❑
Wind Speed _____ Wind Direction _____
High Temperature _____ Low Temperature _____
Plants in Bloom: _____
Other Notes:_____
_____

March 15:
Rainfall _____ Sunny ❑ Overcast ❑
Wind Speed _____ Wind Direction _____
High Temperature _____ Low Temperature _____
Plants in Bloom: _____
Other Notes:_____

_____

April 1:
Rainfall _____ Sunny ❑ Overcast ❑
Wind Speed _____ Wind Direction _____
High Temperature _____ Low Temperature _____
Plants in Bloom: _____
Other Notes:_____

_____

April 15:
Rainfall _____ Sunny ❑ Overcast ❑
Wind Speed _____ Wind Direction _____
High Temperature _____ Low Temperature _____
Plants in Bloom: _____
Other Notes:_____

_____

May 1:
Rainfall _____ Sunny ❑ Overcast ❑
Wind Speed _____ Wind Direction _____
High Temperature _____ Low Temperature _____
Plants in Bloom: _____
Other Notes:_____

_____

May 15:
Rainfall _____ Sunny ❑ Overcast ❑
Wind Speed _____ Wind Direction _____
High Temperature _____ Low Temperature _____
Plants in Bloom: _____
Other Notes:_____

_____

June 1:
Rainfall _____ Sunny ❑ Overcast ❑
Wind Speed _____ Wind Direction _____
High Temperature _____ Low Temperature _____
Plants in Bloom: _____
Other Notes:_____
_____

June 15:
Rainfall _____ Sunny ❑ Overcast ❑
Wind Speed _____ Wind Direction _____
High Temperature _____ Low Temperature _____
Plants in Bloom: _____
Other Notes:_____
_____

July 1:
Rainfall _____ Sunny ❑ Overcast ❑
Wind Speed _____ Wind Direction _____
High Temperature _____ Low Temperature _____
Plants in Bloom: _____
Other Notes:_____
_____

July 15:
Rainfall _____ Sunny ❑ Overcast ❑
Wind Speed _____ Wind Direction _____
High Temperature _____ Low Temperature _____
Plants in Bloom: _____
Other Notes:_____
_____

August 1:
Rainfall _____ Sunny ❑ Overcast ❑
Wind Speed _____ Wind Direction _____
High Temperature _____ Low Temperature _____
Plants in Bloom: _____
Other Notes:_____
_____

August 15:

Rainfall _____ Sunny ❑ Overcast ❑

Wind Speed _____ Wind Direction _____

High Temperature _____ Low Temperature _____

Plants in Bloom: _____

Other Notes:_____

_____

September 1:

Rainfall _____ Sunny ❑ Overcast ❑

Wind Speed _____ Wind Direction _____

High Temperature _____ Low Temperature _____

Plants in Bloom: _____

Other Notes:_____

_____

September 15:

Rainfall _____ Sunny ❑ Overcast ❑

Wind Speed _____ Wind Direction _____

High Temperature _____ Low Temperature _____

Plants in Bloom: _____

Other Notes:_____

_____

October 1:

Rainfall _____ Sunny ❑ Overcast ❑

Wind Speed _____ Wind Direction _____

High Temperature _____ Low Temperature _____

Plants in Bloom: _____

Other Notes:_____

_____

October 15:

Rainfall _____ Sunny ❑ Overcast ❑

Wind Speed _____ Wind Direction _____

High Temperature _____ Low Temperature _____

Plants in Bloom: _____

Other Notes:_____

_____

November 1:
Rainfall _____ Sunny ❑ Overcast ❑
Wind Speed _____ Wind Direction _____
High Temperature _____ Low Temperature _____
Plants in Bloom: _____
Other Notes:_____
_____

November 15:
Rainfall _____ Sunny ❑ Overcast ❑
Wind Speed _____ Wind Direction _____
High Temperature _____ Low Temperature _____
Plants in Bloom: _____
Other Notes:_____
_____

December 1:
Rainfall _____ Sunny ❑ Overcast ❑
Wind Speed _____ Wind Direction _____
High Temperature _____ Low Temperature _____
Plants in Bloom: _____
Other Notes:_____
_____

December 15:
Rainfall _____ Sunny ❑ Overcast ❑
Wind Speed _____ Wind Direction _____
High Temperature _____ Low Temperature _____
Plants in Bloom: _____
Other Notes:_____
_____

AREA THREE TOTALS
Rainfall _____
Date of Most Rainfall _____

Days of Sun _____
Days of Rain _____

Highest Temperature _____
Date of Highest Temperature _____

Lowest Temperature _____
Date of Lowest Temperature _____

Other Notes:_____
_____

Area Four: _____

Place your buildings and out structures along the edges, leaving the graph area for yard shape and size. One inch = one foot.

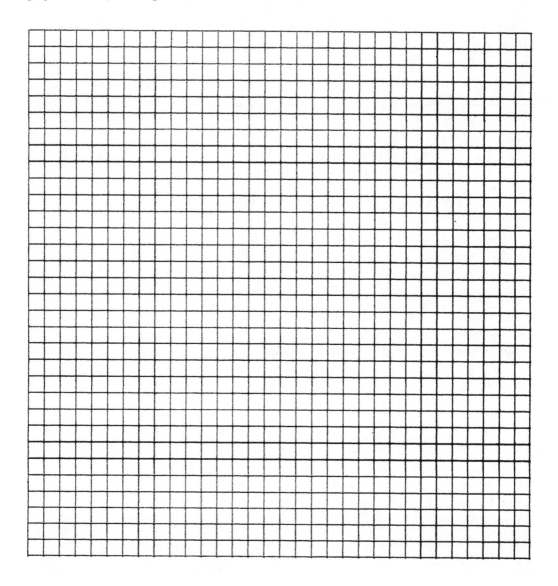

January 1:
Rainfall _____ Sunny ❑ Overcast ❑
Wind Speed _____ Wind Direction _____
High Temperature _____ Low Temperature _____
Plants in Bloom: _____
Other Notes:_____
_____

January 15:
Rainfall _____ Sunny ❑ Overcast ❑
Wind Speed _____ Wind Direction _____
High Temperature _____ Low Temperature _____
Plants in Bloom: _____
Other Notes:_____
_____

February 1:
Rainfall _____ Sunny ❑ Overcast ❑
Wind Speed _____ Wind Direction _____
High Temperature _____ Low Temperature _____
Plants in Bloom: _____
Other Notes:_____
_____

February 15:
Rainfall _____ Sunny ❑ Overcast ❑
Wind Speed _____ Wind Direction _____
High Temperature _____ Low Temperature _____
Plants in Bloom: _____
Other Notes:_____
_____

March 1:
Rainfall _____ Sunny ❑ Overcast ❑
Wind Speed _____ Wind Direction _____
High Temperature _____ Low Temperature _____
Plants in Bloom: _____
Other Notes:_____
_____

March 15:

Rainfall _____ Sunny ❑ Overcast ❑

Wind Speed _____ Wind Direction _____

High Temperature _____ Low Temperature _____

Plants in Bloom: _____

Other Notes:_____

_____

April 1:

Rainfall _____ Sunny ❑ Overcast ❑

Wind Speed _____ Wind Direction _____

High Temperature _____ Low Temperature _____

Plants in Bloom: _____

Other Notes:_____

_____

April 15:

Rainfall _____ Sunny ❑ Overcast ❑

Wind Speed _____ Wind Direction _____

High Temperature _____ Low Temperature _____

Plants in Bloom: _____

Other Notes:_____

_____

May 1:

Rainfall _____ Sunny ❑ Overcast ❑

Wind Speed _____ Wind Direction _____

High Temperature _____ Low Temperature _____

Plants in Bloom: _____

Other Notes:_____

_____

May 15:

Rainfall _____ Sunny ❑ Overcast ❑

Wind Speed _____ Wind Direction _____

High Temperature _____ Low Temperature _____

Plants in Bloom: _____

Other Notes:_____

_____

June 1:

Rainfall _____ Sunny ❑ Overcast ❑

Wind Speed _____ Wind Direction _____

High Temperature _____ Low Temperature _____

Plants in Bloom: _____

Other Notes:_____

_____

June 15:

Rainfall _____ Sunny ❑ Overcast ❑

Wind Speed _____ Wind Direction _____

High Temperature _____ Low Temperature _____

Plants in Bloom: _____

Other Notes:_____

_____

July 1:

Rainfall _____ Sunny ❑ Overcast ❑

Wind Speed _____ Wind Direction _____

High Temperature _____ Low Temperature _____

Plants in Bloom: _____

Other Notes:_____

_____

July 15:

Rainfall _____ Sunny ❑ Overcast ❑

Wind Speed _____ Wind Direction _____

High Temperature _____ Low Temperature _____

Plants in Bloom: _____

Other Notes:_____

_____

August 1:

Rainfall _____ Sunny ❑ Overcast ❑

Wind Speed _____ Wind Direction _____

High Temperature _____ Low Temperature _____

Plants in Bloom: _____

Other Notes:_____

_____

August 15:
Rainfall _____ Sunny ❑ Overcast ❑
Wind Speed _____ Wind Direction _____
High Temperature _____ Low Temperature _____
Plants in Bloom: _____
Other Notes: _____

_____

September 1:
Rainfall _____ Sunny ❑ Overcast ❑
Wind Speed _____ Wind Direction _____
High Temperature _____ Low Temperature _____
Plants in Bloom: _____
Other Notes: _____

_____

September 15:
Rainfall _____ Sunny ❑ Overcast ❑
Wind Speed _____ Wind Direction _____
High Temperature _____ Low Temperature _____
Plants in Bloom: _____
Other Notes: _____

_____

October 1:
Rainfall _____ Sunny ❑ Overcast ❑
Wind Speed _____ Wind Direction _____
High Temperature _____ Low Temperature _____
Plants in Bloom: _____
Other Notes: _____

_____

October 15:
Rainfall _____ Sunny ❑ Overcast ❑
Wind Speed _____ Wind Direction _____
High Temperature _____ Low Temperature _____
Plants in Bloom: _____
Other Notes: _____

_____

November 1:

Rainfall _____ Sunny ❑ Overcast ❑

Wind Speed _____ Wind Direction _____

High Temperature _____ Low Temperature _____

Plants in Bloom: _____

Other Notes:_____

_____

November 15:

Rainfall _____ Sunny ❑ Overcast ❑

Wind Speed _____ Wind Direction _____

High Temperature _____ Low Temperature _____

Plants in Bloom: _____

Other Notes:_____

_____

December 1:

Rainfall _____ Sunny ❑ Overcast ❑

Wind Speed _____ Wind Direction _____

High Temperature _____ Low Temperature _____

Plants in Bloom: _____

Other Notes:_____

_____

December 15:

Rainfall _____ Sunny ❑ Overcast ❑

Wind Speed _____ Wind Direction _____

High Temperature _____ Low Temperature _____

Plants in Bloom: _____

Other Notes:_____

_____

AREA FOUR TOTALS

Rainfall _____
Date of Most Rainfall _____

Days of Sun _____
Days of Rain _____

Highest Temperature _____
Date of Highest Temperature _____

Lowest Temperature _____
Date of Lowest Temperature _____

Other Notes:_____
_____

Area Five: _____

Place your buildings and out structures along the edges, leaving the graph area for yard shape and size. One inch = one foot.

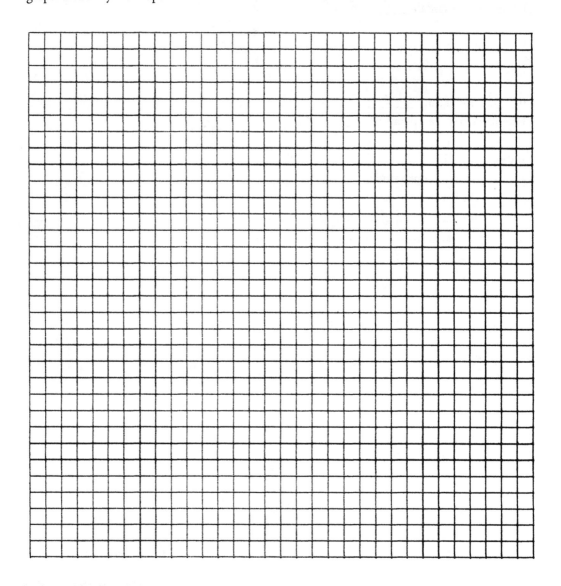

January 1:
Rainfall _____ Sunny ❑ Overcast ❑
Wind Speed _____ Wind Direction _____
High Temperature _____ Low Temperature _____
Plants in Bloom: _____
Other Notes:_____
_____

January 15:
Rainfall _____ Sunny ❑ Overcast ❑
Wind Speed _____ Wind Direction _____
High Temperature _____ Low Temperature _____
Plants in Bloom: _____
Other Notes:_____
_____

February 1:
Rainfall _____ Sunny ❑ Overcast ❑
Wind Speed _____ Wind Direction _____
High Temperature _____ Low Temperature _____
Plants in Bloom: _____
Other Notes:_____
_____

February 15:
Rainfall _____ Sunny ❑ Overcast ❑
Wind Speed _____ Wind Direction _____
High Temperature _____ Low Temperature _____
Plants in Bloom: _____
Other Notes:_____
_____

March 1:
Rainfall _____ Sunny ❑ Overcast ❑
Wind Speed _____ Wind Direction _____
High Temperature _____ Low Temperature _____
Plants in Bloom: _____
Other Notes:_____
_____

March 15:

Rainfall _____ Sunny ❑ Overcast ❑

Wind Speed _____ Wind Direction _____

High Temperature _____ Low Temperature _____

Plants in Bloom: _____

Other Notes:_____

_____

April 1:

Rainfall _____ Sunny ❑ Overcast ❑

Wind Speed _____ Wind Direction _____

High Temperature _____ Low Temperature _____

Plants in Bloom: _____

Other Notes:_____

_____

April 15:

Rainfall _____ Sunny ❑ Overcast ❑

Wind Speed _____ Wind Direction _____

High Temperature _____ Low Temperature _____

Plants in Bloom: _____

Other Notes:_____

_____

May 1:

Rainfall _____ Sunny ❑ Overcast ❑

Wind Speed _____ Wind Direction _____

High Temperature _____ Low Temperature _____

Plants in Bloom: _____

Other Notes:_____

_____

May 15:

Rainfall _____ Sunny ❑ Overcast ❑

Wind Speed _____ Wind Direction _____

High Temperature _____ Low Temperature _____

Plants in Bloom: _____

Other Notes:_____

_____

June 1:
Rainfall _____ Sunny ❏ Overcast ❏
Wind Speed _____ Wind Direction _____
High Temperature _____ Low Temperature _____
Plants in Bloom: _____
Other Notes:_____
_____

June 15:
Rainfall _____ Sunny ❏ Overcast ❏
Wind Speed _____ Wind Direction _____
High Temperature _____ Low Temperature _____
Plants in Bloom: _____
Other Notes:_____
_____

July 1:
Rainfall _____ Sunny ❏ Overcast ❏
Wind Speed _____ Wind Direction _____
High Temperature _____ Low Temperature _____
Plants in Bloom: _____
Other Notes:_____
_____

July 15:
Rainfall _____ Sunny ❏ Overcast ❏
Wind Speed _____ Wind Direction _____
High Temperature _____ Low Temperature _____
Plants in Bloom: _____
Other Notes:_____
_____

August 1:
Rainfall _____ Sunny ❏ Overcast ❏
Wind Speed _____ Wind Direction _____
High Temperature _____ Low Temperature _____
Plants in Bloom: _____
Other Notes:_____
_____

August 15:
Rainfall _____ Sunny ❑ Overcast ❑
Wind Speed _____ Wind Direction _____
High Temperature _____ Low Temperature _____
Plants in Bloom: _____
Other Notes:_____

_____

September 1:
Rainfall _____ Sunny ❑ Overcast ❑
Wind Speed _____ Wind Direction _____
High Temperature _____ Low Temperature _____
Plants in Bloom: _____
Other Notes:_____

_____

September 15:
Rainfall _____ Sunny ❑ Overcast ❑
Wind Speed _____ Wind Direction _____
High Temperature _____ Low Temperature _____
Plants in Bloom: _____
Other Notes:_____

_____

October 1:
Rainfall _____ Sunny ❑ Overcast ❑
Wind Speed _____ Wind Direction _____
High Temperature _____ Low Temperature _____
Plants in Bloom: _____
Other Notes:_____

_____

October 15:
Rainfall _____ Sunny ❑ Overcast ❑
Wind Speed _____ Wind Direction _____
High Temperature _____ Low Temperature _____
Plants in Bloom: _____
Other Notes:_____

_____

November 1:
Rainfall _____ Sunny ❏ Overcast ❏
Wind Speed _____ Wind Direction _____
High Temperature _____ Low Temperature _____
Plants in Bloom: _____
Other Notes:_____
_____

November 15:
Rainfall _____ Sunny ❏ Overcast ❏
Wind Speed _____ Wind Direction _____
High Temperature _____ Low Temperature _____
Plants in Bloom: _____
Other Notes:_____
_____

December 1:
Rainfall _____ Sunny ❏ Overcast ❏
Wind Speed _____ Wind Direction _____
High Temperature _____ Low Temperature _____
Plants in Bloom: _____
Other Notes:_____
_____

December 15:
Rainfall _____ Sunny ❏ Overcast ❏
Wind Speed _____ Wind Direction _____
High Temperature _____ Low Temperature _____
Plants in Bloom: _____
Other Notes:_____
_____

AREA FIVE TOTALS

Rainfall _____
Date of Most Rainfall _____

Days of Sun _____
Days of Rain _____

Highest Temperature _____
Date of Highest Temperature _____

Lowest Temperature _____
Date of Lowest Temperature _____

Other Notes:_____
_____

Area Six: _____

Place your buildings and out structures along the edges, leaving the graph area for yard shape and size. One inch = one foot

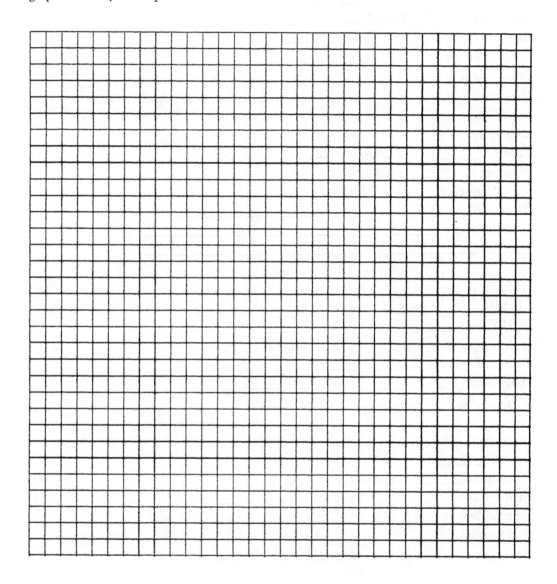

January 1:
Rainfall _____ Sunny ❏ Overcast ❏
Wind Speed _____ Wind Direction _____
High Temperature _____ Low Temperature _____
Plants in Bloom: _____
Other Notes:_____
_____

January 15:
Rainfall _____ Sunny ❏ Overcast ❏
Wind Speed _____ Wind Direction _____
High Temperature _____ Low Temperature _____
Plants in Bloom: _____
Other Notes:_____
_____

February 1:
Rainfall _____ Sunny ❏ Overcast ❏
Wind Speed _____ Wind Direction _____
High Temperature _____ Low Temperature _____
Plants in Bloom: _____
Other Notes:_____
_____

February 15:
Rainfall _____ Sunny ❏ Overcast ❏
Wind Speed _____ Wind Direction _____
High Temperature _____ Low Temperature _____
Plants in Bloom: _____
Other Notes:_____
_____

March 1:
Rainfall _____ Sunny ❏ Overcast ❏
Wind Speed _____ Wind Direction _____
High Temperature _____ Low Temperature _____
Plants in Bloom: _____
Other Notes:_____
_____

March 15:
Rainfall _____ Sunny ❏ Overcast ❏
Wind Speed _____ Wind Direction _____
High Temperature _____ Low Temperature _____
Plants in Bloom: _____
Other Notes:_____
_____

April 1:
Rainfall _____ Sunny ❏ Overcast ❏
Wind Speed _____ Wind Direction _____
High Temperature _____ Low Temperature _____
Plants in Bloom: _____
Other Notes:_____
_____

April 15:
Rainfall _____ Sunny ❏ Overcast ❏
Wind Speed _____ Wind Direction _____
High Temperature _____ Low Temperature _____
Plants in Bloom: _____
Other Notes:_____
_____

May 1:
Rainfall _____ Sunny ❏ Overcast ❏
Wind Speed _____ Wind Direction _____
High Temperature _____ Low Temperature _____
Plants in Bloom: _____
Other Notes:_____
_____

May 15:
Rainfall _____ Sunny ❏ Overcast ❏
Wind Speed _____ Wind Direction _____
High Temperature _____ Low Temperature _____
Plants in Bloom: _____
Other Notes:_____
_____

June 1:
Rainfall _____ Sunny ❑ Overcast ❑
Wind Speed _____ Wind Direction _____
High Temperature _____ Low Temperature _____
Plants in Bloom: _____
Other Notes:_____
_____

June 15:
Rainfall _____ Sunny ❑ Overcast ❑
Wind Speed _____ Wind Direction _____
High Temperature _____ Low Temperature _____
Plants in Bloom: _____
Other Notes:_____
_____

July 1:
Rainfall _____ Sunny ❑ Overcast ❑
Wind Speed _____ Wind Direction _____
High Temperature _____ Low Temperature _____
Plants in Bloom: _____
Other Notes:_____
_____

July 15:
Rainfall _____ Sunny ❑ Overcast ❑
Wind Speed _____ Wind Direction _____
High Temperature _____ Low Temperature _____
Plants in Bloom: _____
Other Notes:_____
_____

August 1:
Rainfall _____ Sunny ❑ Overcast ❑
Wind Speed _____ Wind Direction _____
High Temperature _____ Low Temperature _____
Plants in Bloom: _____
Other Notes:_____
_____

August 15:
Rainfall _____ Sunny ❑ Overcast ❑
Wind Speed _____ Wind Direction _____
High Temperature _____ Low Temperature _____
Plants in Bloom: _____
Other Notes:_____
_____

September 1:
Rainfall _____ Sunny ❑ Overcast ❑
Wind Speed _____ Wind Direction _____
High Temperature _____ Low Temperature _____
Plants in Bloom: _____
Other Notes:_____
_____

September 15:
Rainfall _____ Sunny ❑ Overcast ❑
Wind Speed _____ Wind Direction _____
High Temperature _____ Low Temperature _____
Plants in Bloom: _____
Other Notes:_____
_____

October 1:
Rainfall _____ Sunny ❑ Overcast ❑
Wind Speed _____ Wind Direction _____
High Temperature _____ Low Temperature _____
Plants in Bloom: _____
Other Notes:_____
_____

October 15:
Rainfall _____ Sunny ❑ Overcast ❑
Wind Speed _____ Wind Direction _____
High Temperature _____ Low Temperature _____
Plants in Bloom: _____
Other Notes:_____
_____

November 1:

Rainfall _____ Sunny ❑ Overcast ❑

Wind Speed _____ Wind Direction _____

High Temperature _____ Low Temperature _____

Plants in Bloom: _____

Other Notes:_____

_____

November 15:

Rainfall _____ Sunny ❑ Overcast ❑

Wind Speed _____ Wind Direction _____

High Temperature _____ Low Temperature _____

Plants in Bloom: _____

Other Notes:_____

_____

December 1:

Rainfall _____ Sunny ❑ Overcast ❑

Wind Speed _____ Wind Direction _____

High Temperature _____ Low Temperature _____

Plants in Bloom: _____

Other Notes:_____

_____

December 15:

Rainfall _____ Sunny ❑ Overcast ❑

Wind Speed _____ Wind Direction _____

High Temperature _____ Low Temperature _____

Plants in Bloom: _____

Other Notes:_____

_____

AREA SIX TOTALS

Rainfall _____
Date of Most Rainfall _____

Days of Sun _____
Days of Rain _____

Highest Temperature _____
Date of Highest Temperature _____

Lowest Temperature _____
Date of Lowest Temperature _____

Other Notes:_____
_____

Once we have mapped our garden and recorded important information, we need to analyze our observations. There are four elements crucial in any garden: soil, sun, water, and wind. Each has its own significance and each affects the garden in its own way. The effects of at least two of these elements are unique in coastal gardens. Inland gardens have no salt water and relatively lesser winds to influence them. Most inland gardens are also not primarily sandy soil. But coastal gardens' proximity to the ocean means that sand, wind and salt are important considerations.

Soil

Soil is not dirt. Dirt is what comes into the house on the bottom of your shoes or on the knees of your jeans. Soil is the medium that supports and nourishes plants in the garden and lawn. Soil is where most plants get their nutrients for growth and development. It not only physically supports plants' root systems, but the makeup of the soil has a direct effect on the nourishment the plant is able to take from it. The texture of the soil affects its porosity, which in turn affects its capacity to hold water. For example, a sandy soil is fast draining, but that also means any excess water may wash away nutrients from the root zone, leaving the plants undernourished. Clay or silt-loam soils, on the other hand, do not drain well. This means the plants get little or no oxygen to their roots. The abundance of water can actually smother a plant. Those of us who water our houseplants too frequently and then wonder why they do not do well have firsthand experience at "smothering" with water. So we need to know the makeup of the soil. Is it mostly sand? On the coast this is certainly possible, but not always the case. We may also have loamy soil from the rivers or clay soil in the nearby mountains.

There is an easy test for you to do at home to find out your soil makeup. Using clean tools and a clean five-gallon bucket, take a trowel-full of soil from about 10 random places in your garden area. Remove any clods of soil; rocks; and any leaves, sticks, or other organic debris. Mix the soil well with your trowel. Now take a straight-sided quart jar with a tight lid—a canning jar is a good choice—and fill the jar about one-third full with the soil. Add another third of clean water, and one-half teaspoon of dishwasher detergent to help break up the soil particles. Replace the lid tightly. Shake the jar vigorously for about two minutes, until the soil has mixed with the water into a slurry of mud. Place the jar in an area where it can sit undisturbed for about 24 hours.

When you return to the jar, the soil will have settled into clearly visible layers. The heaviest particles will be sand and they will have settled

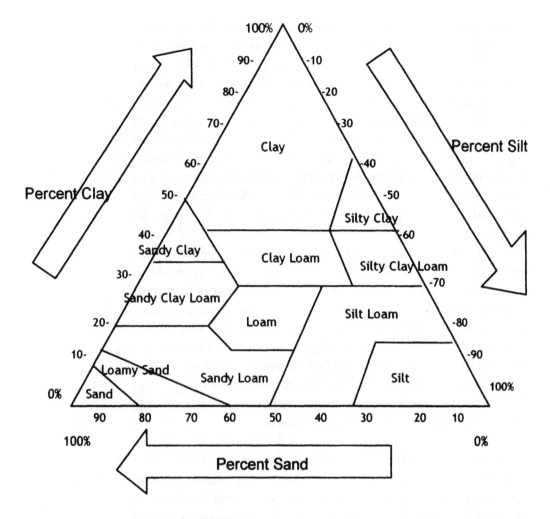

to the bottom. The lightest particles are clay and they will be floating on the top. In between you will see a silt or loam layer. With a ruler, measure the materials in the jar from top to bottom. Now measure each individual layer. Divide the layer's inches by the total inches to find the percentage of each layer. Above is a Soil Texture Chart in the shape of a triangle. By finding the values of the percentages, you can locate them on the soil triangle and figure out the soil type you have. The smallest corners of the chart are Sand and Silt. The mixtures make up most of the middle of the triangle. If you are lucky enough to have silt-loam soil, it will support water and nutrients easier than the clay or sandy soils. The delineation between layers may be so obvious that you will not need the Soil Texture Chart to figure out your percentage.

We also need to know the soil's pH and nutrient makeup. The soil pH test can be done using kits available in most garden centers. All you need is a kit, distilled water, and a sample of soil from the bucket you collected to determine soil type. Directions are on each kit. The nutrient makeup is more complicated to test and should be tested by a laboratory. Check with your county extension agent to find addresses of companies in your area that will test your soil. Most tests run in the $39 to $45 range, but you only need to test your soil about every five years. Often for a small additional charge, the laboratory will be able to tell you what to do to correct your soil so it will support whatever you want to grow there. You can go back to your bucket of soil that you collected for the soil-type test and use the left-over soil from the bucket to send to the laboratory. They will only need a small sample. Most soil test kits come with a small vial or plastic bag to return to the laboratory for analysis.

When you send your soil, be certain to send the paperwork to go with it. They will want to know what you are testing for. Some things are more crucial than others. For example, you will want to know your soil's pH and if your soil is high or low in phosphorous, potassium, boron, and magnesium. You won't need the nitrogen level as that changes with each rainfall. Also among the questions will be what you want to plant in that garden: vegetables or flowers, fruit trees or roses. They all have different needs. The laboratory will return the analysis along with recommendations about the proper amounts of fertilizer to provide nutrients to the plants you have chosen.

An important thing to remember when dealing with soil is that no matter its makeup—clay or sand, silt or loam—it can always benefit from amendment with organic matter. This basically means any material coming from a living source like compost, ground-up bark, or processed steer manure. Professional gardeners recommend a ratio of one-third organic matter to two thirds basic soil, no matter what the soil texture is like. In your garden plans, then, you should include a compost pile, the easiest and least expensive way to get organic matter. We will discuss compost in a later chapter.

While waiting for the results of your soil test to arrive from the laboratory by return mail, let's explore the rest of the garden.

Sun

Sun—or lack of it—is also an important component of garden success. Where does the sun rise? Does your yard have an unobstructed view of the sun all day? If it gets at least six hours of full sun in the summer, that's considered full sun. If it doesn't get any sun, that's considered full shade. There are many variations in between, from part sun to part shade, and this will be important to most of your plants. There are very few varieties of flora that will be able to grow in full sun *or* full shade.

Some will be okay in between, but most like it one way or the other. Vegetables and roses always do best in full sun. Hostas and most ferns prefer moderate shade. Think of what grows in the forest, and you will have a good start on deep shade plants.

The sun/shade issue will change throughout the year. For example, if there are deciduous trees around, they will mean summer shade but winter sun. This may not be as much of an issue as you think because we get less sun in the winter. So shade lovers are not usually harmed by the winter sun. Most perennials are dormant by then anyway.

The arc the sun takes across the sky in each season will be important when planning your garden. We moved into our home in December and I was convinced I would need to plant shade-loving plants in my yard. But by the time July rolled around, I was looking for some shelter from the hot summer sun. The sun's path had come so far north that my garden was almost full sun by mid June. So try to note that on your workbook maps. You may try using a different colored pencil to mark the sun's path in each season. If you do this, be sure to label each path as to its season, or make a key in the map's corner as to which color represents which season. Remember: Patience!

Water and Salt Water

For our purposes, the term water not only refers to rainfall, although that is certainly an issue in coastal gardens, but irrigation as well. Recently, we have gotten most of our rainfall from November through March, and very little in June, July, and August. Some regions of the Oregon/Washington/British Columbia coast are even considered to be drought areas. It is difficult to find plants that like a lot of winter rain and not much in the summer. So when we talk of "water" we must also consider a water source for those possible summer droughts. Is there a hose bib near the garden? If not, how costly would it be to install one? Will hoses reach? Will you be carrying watering cans to the vegetable patch? (Buckets of water are heavy, so this is not always a good option. Is a drip irrigation system an alternative?) Will your soil type need frequent water or not much at all? Most plants will need only about an inch of irrigation each week. In sandy soil, any more water will leach away the nutrients. Any less will not be sufficient. Silt or clay soil will hold two inches of water or more, so you may need to correct the irrigation flow so the water is absorbed more slowly to prevent it from running off and eroding the topsoil, or worse, smothering the plants as we discussed previously.

A soil that stays wet in the spring and summer will be damaged if you try to work in it too soon. Seeds are also less likely to germinate in cold, wet soil. If you have amended your soil with organic matter and it still stays wet, try using raised beds or creating drainage using a slight slope. Be sure to check with local officials, though, to see where it is proper for the water to be channeled.

Salt and salt water can have a detrimental effect on a coastal garden, but, because of the varying degrees of exposure to the ocean, that effect will vary. Some gardens abut the dunes. Others are a few feet back from the ocean shore, while still others are miles away, protected by the mountains, buildings, and forests.

We can all grasp the concept that salt water is very damaging to most plants. Their cells are not designed to process water with high salt contents. It can be deadly to their roots and impede their photosynthesis processes. And yet, there are those shore pines and beach grasses that do very well in salt spray. What does that tell us?

Mother Nature is a wonderful force. Over millennia human beings have evolved from uncivilized, hairy animals to the sophisticated, refined, intelligent creatures we are today. We developed opposing thumbs and learned to walk upright. Plants have evolved, too. Since they couldn't get up and move away from the oceans, they had to find ways to process salt water and adapt their food-making cells to absorb it. This was not an overnight progression, but it resulted in some pretty tough plants. Their evolution tells us that if we have a garden that will get a fair amount of salt spray, we are best to look to the natives such as yarrow, beach grass, Sitka spruce, madrone, salal, and manzanita to include in our design.

We also have the option of screening for the salt spray by using fences and native trees and shrubs. This of course won't eliminate salt from the air if you live close to the ocean, but it can reduce the harsh effects of the salt by creating more favorable microclimates.

If you are far enough away from the ocean that you aren't affected by the salt water and salt spray, the realm of plants you can use for your garden increases dramatically.

Wind

One of the most destructive aspects of living along the coast is the wind. Generally the summer winds come from the north and the winter winds from the south, but this is not always the case. The strength of the winds is an issue as well. It is not unusual to have winds reaching 50 or 60 miles per hour, or even stronger. So plants chosen for a windy coast will have to be sturdy and wind tolerant. Preferably they will also have a strong root system that will keep them from being blown over. With the wind comes the sea spray as we have already discussed, so you may want to choose those natives that have adapted to salt spray and

wind if you live in an exposed area. When you are making your garden graphs, be sure to indicate from which direction the winds come and if they will affect your garden. A weather vane may be helpful. Many homes and out buildings have been constructed in such a way that they will act as a natural screen from the wind.

Fence styled to allow passage of wind

If you want to use windscreens or wooden fences to block the wind, do not make them solid structures. The wind will fly over the fence and make the area at the base even colder. The wind needs to pass through, so leave some space between slats. An alternating slat fence is an ideal design, as are ones with cutout designs to allow the wind to pass through.

Many trees, such as the Shore pine (*Pinus contorta contorta*), are already adapted for coastal use and have unusual shapes because the winds have formed their growth habits. They look windblown because they are.

STEP FOUR: LOCATION, LOCATION, LOCATION . . .

When you think about locating a vegetable garden, think first about how far you want it to be from the house. If you live on a slope, will you be walking uphill to get to the garden? Or uphill to get back to the house or shed? All of this will, of course, depend on which areas get the most sun or have the most shade.

When you think about locating flower beds, remember you will probably want a view of them from inside the house as well as the approach to the house. What kind of a view do you have? If your view is a lovely one, you won't want to plant large trees that will impede the scene. Instead, use that view as a backdrop and incorporate elements that complement the scene rather than detract from it. If your view is less than ideal, what kind of screening will your garden need? You may consider a fence, hedge, or those large trees.

Other things to consider when you decide the location for your garden might be: Who will be using your garden? Children, grandchildren, and pets will appreciate a play area. Even if that's not an issue, do you want a bench or comfortable chairs in which to spend a lazy summer afternoon? Back to your graph pages to decide if the area should be in a sunny location or tucked in a spot under a tree or an arbor. You will want a nice view from the bench as well. Flower beds, the ocean, or the mountains are much nicer for reflection than the back of the garage or the compost pile. Seating areas should be protected from the wind.

Will you be barbequing and dining outside? Ideally, a grill and picnic area would be beside the house and close to kitchen access as well. Again, keep them sheltered from the wind. For dining areas, a sunny location is best for our cool summers. Coastal evenings are chilly for dining out, and if your table is in the shade, it can be downright cold. A windbreak or fire pit are useful, but ask yourself how much they will heat the area. Perhaps a glassed-in picnic area would be more useful for exterior dining.

. . . Size, Size, Size

When you are thinking about the size of your future garden, consider who will be doing most of the work. How much time, energy, and money do you have to devote? This is a crucial decision in any garden design, but especially on the Washington and Oregon coasts where many of the homes are for part-time use only. If you won't be in residence each week to tend to the gardens and you can't or don't want to hire a professional to care for them, best rethink having high-maintenance plants like roses. On the other hand, if you are retired, living full time at the coast, enjoy gardening—even weeding—and are physically able to do it, you are limited only by the size of your property.

One of the most difficult things for a novice gardener to decide is the theme or focus of their garden. Even many experienced gardeners have a difficult time finding a focus. We shop in nurseries and fall in love with plants we see with little regard to where it will fit into our existing gardens. So the poor plant is purchased and then ends up being stuck in a totally inappropriate spot. We all have done this. We are vigilant and we pack our plants so carefully in the car, making certain the pots will not tip over on the way home. We line our trunks with plastic so that water from the plant doesn't drip and spoil our trunk mat. Once home, we carefully remove the plant from the car and bring it into the yard. And then we stand with it in our arms and look around for the best place. We stroll here and there, turning in small circles to view the area from different angles. And when we find the right spot—for us, not necessarily the plant—we dig a hole, plop the plant into it and water it thoroughly. Did we even bother to read the tag that said "full sun" or "prefers well-drained soil?" In three weeks we can't understand why the little thing looks so frail and wilted. Off we go, back to the nursery to either complain or buy another specimen.

Garden design is often left to the professional simply because it is too daunting a task for most people to undertake. One of the easiest ways is to sit with a nice gardening magazine or book featuring color photographs, and start noticing what catches your eye. Do you prefer formal, groomed gardens with their shaped hedges and topiary, everything standing in a straight line? Perhaps the cluttered and blowsy look of the English Cottage Garden is more appealing. Another type of garden especially popular on the West Coast is the Japanese or Zen garden, with its stark lines and simplicity of form and color. If you are working with an old magazine, clip out your favorite photos and place them in a folder or glue them onto a scrapbook page. Be sure to include the original captions in case you want to replicate the plants in your own garden later. By setting the photographs side by side, you will begin to see a pattern of what you prefer. There is also very good, easy-to-use computer software available that can help you visualize and plan your garden.

There are always more decisions when you think about design. Are you looking for masses of color all summer? That will most likely require the purchase of annuals each spring. If you prefer a little less groomed look, you might prefer perennials that will bloom for a set amount of time and then fade into the background for the rest of the year. Either garden can be lovely; it is just a matter of budget and personal preference.

In the following chapters, we'll explore some possible themes for coastal gardens.

MAINTENANCE

There are many aspects of planning and planting a new garden. We have already discussed the type and quality of your soil, the amount of sunlight available, the amount of accessibility of water both as rain and through irrigation, the slope of the site, the proximity to the ocean and to the mountains as being important factors.

Perhaps something most gardeners, especially those who are new to the coast as well as new to gardening, forget about is the maintenance required for a garden. Any gardener who has looked longingly at a magazine or book with photographs of beautiful gardens has dreamed of having those beautiful gardens in their yards. Ah, but do we have the time?

Believe it or not, planning and installing a garden are the least time consuming stages of a gardening project. You will have spent hours designing the site, choosing plants, preparing the soil. But a garden is a life-long endeavor of love. If you create a garden that is too large, you will feel frustrated when you can not find the time or energy to get out and weed it, deadhead the flowers, or bed the garden down for winter. If you fashion a garden that is too small, you will find yourself regretting that you didn't make it larger. Like Goldilocks, you need a garden that is "just right."

The mistake of designing too small a garden is easier to correct than making one that is too large. Providing you have the space, you can always enlarge it. Better to start small and see how much you can comfortably handle before going to a larger plot. It is certainly more difficult to shrink a garden to a manageable size. So while you are evaluating all the other conditions of your site, take a few minutes to evaluate your time and your energy level.

There are a few questions to ask yourself that will help assess maintenance. How much time will I have on a daily basis to devote to tasks like deadheading? How much time will I be able to devote on a weekly basis to weeding and mowing the lawn? Will I have time in the fall to clean out the garden beds, rake the fallen leaves, cut back the wilted perennials, remove the annuals and move the plants that need to be winterized indoors? Will I have time in the spring to again clean out the beds and cut back the perennial grasses? Will I want to be spending time before work or after work and on weekends all summer to tend to what needs to be done? Will anyone else in the family be helping?

Many retired individuals love to be in their gardens when they are no longer working and have the time to devote to them. But those retired gardeners may also want to travel in the summer, spring or fall, making gardening tasks a lower priority.

Then there is the problem of energy. Ask yourself: What is my age level and how physically fit am I? How is my back? How are my knees, elbows, hands, and wrists? Am I willing and able to dig with a shovel or a trowel? Can I stoop? Can I get down on my hands and knees to weed? Once I have gotten down to weed, can I get up? Will I be able to bend over all those coreopsis to deadhead them on an almost daily basis in August? Do I have the ability and equipment to mow a large lawn?

What are your priorities with the garden? Do you like a vast expanse of lawn? Or just a tiny bit for the dog to lay in the sun? Do you enjoy weeding? Deadheading? Cutting flowers to bring inside? Or are flowers not your thing? Would you prefer the simplicity of a Zen Garden, which we discuss in chapter 2?

Be realistic. And be brutally honest. Because if you cannot physically do any of these ordinary tasks, or if you do not like the mundane chores involved, perhaps you should reevaluate a large garden. A small raised bed for a few vegetables or flowers may be just what you need instead. You can also construct raised beds that are tall enough to allow you to stand and weed.

A low-maintenance garden is also a possibility for a busy person or an older one. Notice I said "low-maintenance" and not "no-maintenance." Except for paving the lawn and painting it green, I can think of no way to eliminate some weeding or mowing of a yard. Even those homeowners on the coast who have put in river rock as a ground cover will have weeds that poke through now and then. But you can choose plants that take less work than others. Roses are "high maintenance" but Echinacea bloom for months with very little tending. Hostas need to be slug-baited regularly but ferns only need to be cut back in the early spring to be happy.

You may have the choice of hiring someone to do your gardening chores for you, and with our busy lifestyles, this may be an appealing option. Treat your garden like you would your home—don't get just anyone off the street to do the work. Ask friends and neighbors for referrals. There are many firms and some individuals who make gardening maintenance a good business. If you see a garden you admire, ask the owner who they employ. You may also want to check with shopkeepers to ask who does the gardening for their business. Choosing a gardening firm from the phone book or classified ads can be problematic, but if this is your only option, be sure to ask for references and then follow up by calling those references. A visit to some of the gardens they tend would not be out of order here, either.

Several states on the coast require licenses for landscape designers or architects but not for people doing maintenance work. Try to find someone with gardening credentials, such as a degree in horticulture or at least several years of gardening experience. You may be able to call the county extension office and get a few suggestions from them. Costs will vary, depending on the expertise for the work needed to be done as well as the geographical area. Northern Californians and Washingtonians should expect to pay more than rural Oregonians, and those closer to large cities will spend more per hour as well. Get a firm price per hour when hiring a regular maintenance person. And please be prompt in paying when they have done the work. They need to make a living, too.

If you are hiring someone to do only a one-time, specific job, get an estimate in writing that spells out exactly what you need done. For a large project, you will want to review bids from at least three firms. Having a list of tasks available to give to the contractor will aid her/him in figuring their bid, but give the same list to each firm. When you receive the bids, compare more than prices. Evaluate materials to be used, the firm's expertise, experience, and references as well as cost. You may not want to choose the lowest bid if the contractor will be using inferior materials or cannot promise either a start date nor a completion date. Again, call the references to avoid any surprises down the road. Check credentials with local authorities, especially if you are having someone build a substantial retaining wall or other large structural project.

By assessing time, energy, and interests, you will more easily be able to decide the size and maintenance requirements of your garden.

PLANNING FOR THE SEASONS

When you are thinking about plants for your new garden space, take a little time to organize those plants into seasonal interest. This concept has become very popular in the last several years and because we have such a long growing time on the coast, you will want to have something of interest in your garden for the entire year. It just won't do to have all the perennials gone from October until February when there are many plants that can fill the voids and give your garden color each month.

Spring and summer are taken care of with the flowering shrubs and perennials that we will discuss in the following chapters. Fall is a little harder because we do not get the cold temperatures that many trees require to colorfully change their leaves. We must accept the fact that we will never have as pretty an autumn as Vermont, New Hampshire, or Pennsylvania, but we can still plan for some oranges and reds in our October landscape.

Vine maples (*Acer circinatum*), katsura trees (*Cercidiphyllum japonicum*), maidenhair trees (*Gingko biloba*) and kousa dogwoods (*Cornus kousa*) are all examples of trees with nice fall color. Planted in a grouping of three or five—if you have space—will give your yard a good splash of color. Doublefile Viburnum (*Viburnum plicatum tomentosum*) and Witch hazels (*Hamamelis* species) are good deciduous shrubs for coastal fall foliage. The 'Profusion' variety of beautyberry (*Callicarpa bodinieri* 'Profusion'), Sarcococca (*Sarcocca ruscifolia*) and Japanese skimmia (*Skimmia japonica*) have nice berries in the autumn, making them first-rate shrub choices for fall and winter interest.

Red-twigged dogwood (*Cornus stolonifera*) or yellow-twigged dogwood (*Cornus stolonifera* 'Flaviramea') give a lot of winter interest once their leaves have fallen. The graceful vase-shaped form of these shrubs takes second place to the color of their branches. In late winter, cut this shrub severely since the new growth has the color. These dogwoods can form large clumps but they can be kept in place by cutting the creeping roots with a spade and by trimming branches that creep along the ground. Share the new plants with friends. Its spreading habit makes this type of dogwood a wonderful plant to hold back hillsides or to use as a screen. They like moist ground and full sun.

Other good coastal shrubs for autumn and winter include heavenly bamboo (*Nandina domestica*), European cranberry bush (*Viburnum opulus*), English holly *(Ilex aquifolium)*, winter daphne (*Daphne odora*), and the cotoneasters.

By using a little preplanning, your gardens can have color and variety enough to make your gardens beautiful in any season.

MY TOOL BUCKET AND POTTING SHED

I have the luxury of having been able to convert an old building on our property into a potting shed. We put windows in it, built a potting bench and added a few shelves and hangers for tools. It is a haven for me, and I always take a deep breath when I walk in the door and enjoy the scent of bark mulch and potting soil. Perfume to my gardener's nose.

If you need to build a potting shed, err on the side of making it larger than you think you will need. I find at least a 10' x 10' shed is necessary once you have a potting bench and the shelves you need for pots and plants in it. You will need a place to store your buckets and a rack to hang rakes, shovels, and pitchforks on. Floor space will be necessary for bags of mulch and soil. A high shelf or locked cabinet is good to have for storing garden chemicals. Even if you are an organic gardener, there will be fertilizers that should be kept out of reach of children and pets.

I also have a bucket of tools that I can carry with me into the garden. I use an old, cleaned-out cat litter bucket because it has a tight-fitting lid. I like a lid because I sometimes work in a drizzle, and I hate to have wet tools. A five-gallon bucket would work just as well without a lid. I also like to have several of the five-gallon buckets to take into the garden while I'm deadheading flowers, collecting weeds, or moving plants. They are often free or inexpensive in the hardware stores and generally have sturdy handles. Anything larger tends to get too heavy when loaded with debris.

In my tool bucket I keep two trowels, a narrow one and a wide one. The narrow one is good for getting into tighter spaces and the broader one I use when digging a hole too small to use a shovel. I also have a forked weeding tool that I use all the time. I bought mine at an antique shop for about five dollars because it has a nice, strong handle and the newer ones just don't have the right feel in my hand. I have a "claw" tool that helps to break up soil as well as rake under shrubs. I have two good pairs of by-pass pruning shears. I like them because they make a clean cut when I am pruning and don't smash the branch as anvil-type pruners tend to do. I have a pair of stainless steel scissors that I use for cutting open bags of mulch as well as deadheading plants. I have a sharp kitchen carving knife that I use to cut roots, loosen dirt around the edges of pots, or cut into sod. There are fancier knives available, but I find my garage sale find works fine for me. I also have two or three pairs of gloves in my bucket at any one time. I used to work bare-handed, but since I am forever picking up slugs, I prefer to be gloved. I like the kind with plastic palms that also have breathable cloth backs. I spend more for my gardening gloves than the ones in "two-for-three-dollars" sales, because I work them hard and want good quality. I have heavy pairs for winter gardening and lightweight ones for summer use.

Also in my bucket are disinfectant wipes. I buy these in the cleaning section of the grocery store and get the ones that kill bacteria. I use these each time I make a pruning cut on a plant with a fungal disease. I also have a spool of twine and a few twist-ties in case I need to tie up a plant to support it.

I wear knee pads with gel inserts to protect my knees while I am gardening. I have gotten to the point I can't do without these anymore. I used to use kneeling pads, but find the knee pads to be more convenient when I am crawling on the ground. A seat that turns upside down to convert to a kneeler would also be a good investment. This would give added support when rising from a kneeling position, too.

In the potting shed, I have a rack with a long-handled but small-headed flower shovel that I use in the perennial beds. I also have a standard shovel for bigger digging projects. I have two small pitchforks that I use when I divide clumps of perennials such as daylilies. I have a heavy-duty garden rake and a lighter-weight leaf rake. A pair of hedge shears and lopping shears are vital for larger jobs, too. I consider all of these tools to be essential.

In the nice-to-have-but-not-necessary category, I would put a gardening apron. I like to have something with big, deep pockets that I can slip a tool into if I need to use both hands to do a certain chore. I have a good, heavy-duty apron that is coated with Teflon so the dirt doesn't stick and it comes out beautifully in the wash. It's a full-front apron, but the carpenters' tool belts would also work as long as the pockets hold enough tools.

When buying new tools, which I sometimes have to do because I lose them or wear them out, I always look for something that has a comfortable feel in my hand. To this end I will sometimes walk around the store for several minutes, holding onto a trowel or a rake, just to test the weight and the grip. Yes, I may look a little silly, but if after 15 minutes of holding a tool it feels too heavy or the grip is too wide and my hand begins to cramp, I know I won't want to use it in the garden either.

Rust. Its not just a disease of roses. On the coast, with the ocean breezes and the winter rains, most steel or iron composite tools will have a tendency to rust. If you are good about keeping your tools clean and dry, you can prolong the life of your tools. After each garden use, wipe any dirt off the tool. If necessary, wash it off with water and dry the tools thoroughly. If I have been working among diseased plants, I also take the time to disinfect my tools with a bleach and water solution after I wash them. About 1 part bleach to 10 parts water will be sufficient. Let them soak in the solution for about 15 minutes. Then dry them and wipe them with oil to protect them from rust. Many people use motor oil for this purpose, but I hate the thought of digging into the soil with a shovel that has motor oil residue on it. So my oil of preference is vegetable oil. I get a large bottle of the least expensive I can find in the grocery store and keep it in the potting shed with a roll of paper towels. After drying the tools, apply the oil with a paper towel and hang them up to dry.

At the end of the season, you may want to take one of your five-gallon buckets and fill it halfway with clean builder's sand. A cup or two of the vegetable oil can be mixed into the sand and your tools stuck into the sand/oil mix for the winter. (If you want to dedicate a bucket just for this purpose, you could leave the sand/oil combination in it year round and stand your tools in it after each use.) The sand helps to clean the tools and the oil will keep them from rusting. In the spring, remove the tools from the sand and wipe them off. You may at this point need to sharpen them. Sharpen the edges of your shovels and trowels for ease of digging.

With this little extra work at the end of each gardening day, you will find your tools will stay cleaner and last longer.

SHOPPING!

In the following chapters we will address themes and forms of gardens that may work for your coastal yard. In each chapter there will be suggested plants that have proven successful in the Pacific Northwest. But since we are discussing the basics, and since we have laid the groundwork for creating a garden, its time to do something fun: shop for plants!

I don't know a "hortiholic" who doesn't drool at the thought of plant shopping. We are so addicted to our hobby that we can't resist a spin by the gardening section of our hardware or even the grocery store. And get a group of us together for a trip to a "real" nursery and we are like kids in a candy store, roaming the aisles, moving from side to side and plant to plant, oohing and aahing. But to be efficient and avoid plant mistakes, we should try to stick to our plan and our plant list. Notice I said "try." It isn't always easy. But just like grocery shopping, if you go with a list of items you are looking for, you will be less likely to submit to impulse buying.

After you have decided on a theme for your garden and have laid out the preliminary plans on your graph pages, you will have made a list of plants that have intrigued you to the point you want to include them in your garden. Hopefully you have already had a soil test done, tilled and amended the soil, and are ready to shop. Set yourself a spending limit and stick to it.

One of the best gardening tips I can give you is to ask friends for recommendations of a nursery in your area. Buying plants that have been raised at the coast gives them—and you—a head start on success. Each state has an association of nursery owners, and I would advise shopping at members' nurseries when possible as these men and women are up-to-date on developments in the industry and are generally conscientious about selling clean, healthy plants. Some nurseries set up display gardens that may inspire ideas for plant combinations as well as indicate how a specific plant grows.

If you can't find the plants you want in a coastal nursery, you might need to go inland for something specific. Again, ask friends to give you recommendations as to where they like to shop. If you have questions as to whether a certain plant will grow at the coast, ask the nursery owner or staff. A good nursery will employ knowledgeable and friendly staff to help you both find plants and tell you about their needs. If any nursery doesn't have a good feeling to it, leave and find somewhere you will feel at ease. You will want to establish a good relationship with a local nursery, and if you don't feel comfortable, you won't want to shop there.

A quick trip around the nursery and its gardens will give you an idea of the layout. Then you can focus on your list and go back to find the

Coastal Gardening in the Pacific Northwest

plants you need. Prices should be clearly marked, as should the plants' names. Look for plant tags and signage that give information such as botanical names, common names, size at maturity, and sun and watering needs. You may need to take along a small notebook and take notes on growing conditions. The notebook also helps should you need to jot down names of potential additions to the garden as you find spots you need to fill in later. This way you can take the information home and do some further research before you purchase a plant that may not work for you.

Look at the plant itself before you buy it. Lift it out of the group, and compare it to the plants around it to see which one looks the healthiest. Ask yourself more questions: Is the growth healthy but not spindly? Are the leaves the color they should be and not yellowing or brown? Are there a lot of leaves that have fallen off? Pass these plants by and try to find others.

Are the roots showing from the bottom drainage holes? This indicates a degree of neglect because the plant needs to be repotted. Most good nurseries won't mind if you lift the plant gently from the pot to check the root growth. The roots should be white and round. Any dark or shriveled roots indicate problems you won't want to deal with. Don't let a slightly root-bound plant put you off, though. Often during the fall planting season, the nurseries put the plants on sale that they didn't have time to properly tend to during the summer. If the plant is slightly root bound, you can make some correction by gently pulling the roots from the dirtball and loosening them before you place it in the ground. However, a pot that is so dense that the roots are solid should be passed by.

You may want to invite a gardening friend—a practical, candid, and patient one—to go shopping with you. We can become so enamored of a plant's attributes that we forget to think of where it fits into our plan. Having someone who can say, "Now where in your shady yard are you going to put that sun-loving plant?" can be invaluable in keeping us from bringing the wrong plant home. They also may bring some insight to plants we would have not otherwise considered. Your friend might be in the market for a new addition to his garden, too, and you can give your perspective as a trade off for his help. And it can make the day more fun.

Lastly, find a quiet corner of the nursery and set together the plants you have chosen in approximately the same layout as they will be in the garden, for example, the large plants in the back, the smaller ones in front. Do you like the color combinations? Consider the foliage as well as the flowers. Some plants have a gray-blue tint to their green while others are more of a chartreuse. These two groups may not look good together. Try to find varieties that have the same color range, all blues or all chartreuse. Light and dark tones and variegation in the leaves, as well as using different leaf shapes, can add interest. You will want the plants to blend well together and not clash.

Visit your local nurseries at several crucial times in the growing season. By visiting in the summer, you will be able to see the growth pattern—whether the plant is small, tall, upright, or bushy. A visit in the fall will give an indication of whether or not the plant has autumn coloration. Fall is also the best time for planting most shrubs and trees, because our cool, wet winters will allow the shrub to adjust to its location, and you won't need to water the new ones as frequently. If your nursery is open during the winter months, stop by to see what shrubs and trees have winter interest. A deciduous azalea, for example, is rather boring in the summer after the spring blooms have faded. But in the fall, the leaves turn a lovely orange, and, for winter interest, you can't beat the gnarled and twisting branches. When you stop by a nursery year round, you will get to know the plants better. I leave my wallet locked in the car trunk, though, because I rarely can leave a nursery without making a purchase. I take a notebook and pen with me instead.

By shopping with your list and a budget, you will come home happier with the plants you have found. And you won't be searching for just the right place to plant them because you will already know where they are going to live in your garden.

PERSONALIZING YOUR GARDEN

Let's discuss personal preference for a moment before we go on. Keep in mind this is your garden. Not your neighbor's, not your friends', and not your mother's. There are a few "design rules" to follow for a pleasing display, but they deal mostly with sizes, shapes, and lights and darks instead of flower color combinations. If you like the combination of orange and pink, don't be put off by someone saying they don't "go" together. I am a firm believer that any flower looks good with any other flower—some just look better than others. A riot of color can be stunning and very cheerful. A monochromatic color scheme can be soothing, and a white garden can be hauntingly beautiful in the moonlight. Neither will be eye catching during the heat of the day, but if you are only home in the evenings, a "moon garden" may be perfect for you. Remember—it is *your* garden.

PLANT LIST

Plants Currently in My Yard

			Date Planted
Keep	Remove	Change	(if known)
❏	❏	❏ _____	_____
❏	❏	❏ _____	_____
❏	❏	❏ _____	_____
❏	❏	❏ _____	_____
❏	❏	❏ _____	_____
❏	❏	❏ _____	_____
❏	❏	❏ _____	_____
❏	❏	❏ _____	_____
❏	❏	❏ _____	_____
❏	❏	❏ _____	_____
❏	❏	❏ _____	_____
❏	❏	❏ _____	_____
❏	❏	❏ _____	_____
❏	❏	❏ _____	_____
❏	❏	❏ _____	_____
❏	❏	❏ _____	_____
❏	❏	❏ _____	_____
❏	❏	❏ _____	_____
❏	❏	❏ _____	_____
❏	❏	❏ _____	_____
❏	❏	❏ _____	_____
❏	❏	❏ _____	_____
❏	❏	❏ _____	_____
❏	❏	❏ _____	_____
❏	❏	❏ _____	_____
❏	❏	❏ _____	_____
❏	❏	❏ _____	_____
❏	❏	❏ _____	_____
❏	❏	❏ _____	_____
❏	❏	❏ _____	_____
❏	❏	❏ _____	_____
❏	❏	❏ _____	_____
❏	❏	❏ _____	_____
❏	❏	❏ _____	_____
❏	❏	❏ _____	_____
❏	❏	❏ _____	_____
❏	❏	❏ _____	_____

PLANT WISH LIST

Area	Name	Quantity	Done	Date Planted
___	_____	_____	❑	_____
___	_____	_____	❑	_____
___	_____	_____	❑	_____
___	_____	_____	❑	_____
___	_____	_____	❑	_____
___	_____	_____	❑	_____
___	_____	_____	❑	_____
___	_____	_____	❑	_____
___	_____	_____	❑	_____
___	_____	_____	❑	_____
___	_____	_____	❑	_____
___	_____	_____	❑	_____
___	_____	_____	❑	_____
___	_____	_____	❑	_____
___	_____	_____	❑	_____
___	_____	_____	❑	_____
___	_____	_____	❑	_____
___	_____	_____	❑	_____
___	_____	_____	❑	_____
___	_____	_____	❑	_____
___	_____	_____	❑	_____
___	_____	_____	❑	_____
___	_____	_____	❑	_____
___	_____	_____	❑	_____
___	_____	_____	❑	_____
___	_____	_____	❑	_____
___	_____	_____	❑	_____
___	_____	_____	❑	_____
___	_____	_____	❑	_____
___	_____	_____	❑	_____
___	_____	_____	❑	_____
___	_____	_____	❑	_____
___	_____	_____	❑	_____
___	_____	_____	❑	_____
___	_____	_____	❑	_____
___	_____	_____	❑	_____
___	_____	_____	❑	_____
___	_____	_____	❑	_____
___	_____	_____	❑	_____
___	_____	_____	❑	_____
___	_____	_____	❑	_____
___	_____	_____	❑	_____

Coastal Gardening in the Pacific Northwest

TWO

DUNE GARDENING

IT MAY SEEM OBVIOUS that the sand is a crucial element when gardening on or near the dunes, but many people do not seem to give their location enough thought. I have seen novice gardeners clear a spot in their coastal yard and make a trip to the nursery, bringing back plants that are pretty and hearty looking but totally inappropriate in sand. As we discussed in the first chapter, you need to know the basic make-up of the soil you will be working with. If you haven't already done the jar test described in chapter 1, this is a good time to get that started so you will know the results in 24 hours.

The previous owner of your home may also have been a gardener and might have already amended the soil. Do the jar test anyway. You may be pleasantly—or unpleasantly—surprised. Just because your soil looks black and rich, doesn't mean it is "good soil." In many places along the North Oregon Coast, for example, the soil has a lot of peat in it. The dark brown or almost black color gives the illusion that the soil is high in nutrients and composted materials. This is partly true . . . peat is made up of decaying matter. On the other hand, think of what grows in a peat bog: not much. It is thick and feels slimy to the touch. Peat supports very few nutrients and no oxygen for the roots of your plants to survive. This type of soil will have to be amended.

If your test results show a high percentage of sand in your soil mix, or if you live on or near a sand dune, you will need to amend the sand with compost. You may at this point also consider making raised beds to better hold the newly composted soil in place.

RAISED BEDS

There are many reasons for using raised beds, not the least of which is the fact that in coastal climates they warm the soil faster and keep it warmer longer into the growing season, allowing for earlier—and longer—plantings. Raised beds can warm the soil as much as five degrees and be ready for planting one to two weeks earlier than if you were planting directly into the ground. And raised beds are not just for vegetables. They can be design elements as a terraced hillside for annual and perennial plants and shrubs. They can be problem solvers for soil that is too sandy or clay that is hard packed. Grasses and mints can be more effectively contained in raised beds. In the winter, drainage is better, and in dry summers, raised beds lend themselves easily to drip irrigation.

An example of an easy-to-make raised bed is to use concrete builders' blocks, stacked in a rectangle or square with corners overlapping. Lay out your bed using string and stakes, making sure the final result will be straight and level and have squared-off corners. Lay one course of blocks all the way around before adding the second course. The subsequent layers should be alternated for more strength and stability of the walls. Cement blocks are heavy enough not to need to be mortared. Keep in mind, using cement blocks will make the soil inside the beds more alkaline because the cement will gradually leach into the soil. Frequent pH tests will be required and the soil amended as necessary. If you are starting with acidic soil, this may be a perfect solution **Raised bed wall**

Coastal Gardening in the Pacific Northwest

for most of your vegetables, which prefer more alkaline soil. Bricks may also be used without the alkaline effect, but they must be secured with mortar because of the tendency of the soil to push away from the center of the beds.

Large stones can also be used for raised beds, dry stacking them to a height of 12 to 18 inches. Be sure to put larger rocks at the base and make the walls sturdy enough to lean on without toppling inward. A stone wall with plants cascading over the sides can be a very pretty effect in a perennial garden.

However, most raised beds are constructed out of wood because of the low cost and the ease of finding materials. Recycled lumber is often available, reducing the cost even further. Use caution when using creosoted railroad ties or landscape timbers chemically treated with arsenates, as these might leach undesirable chemicals into the soil. This is especially harmful when planting vegetables into the raised beds. Cedar, pressure-treated lumber, or redwood will last longer than most other woods, but even these will rot over time. Long-lasting plastic landscape timbers are becoming more available and have the added benefits of coming from recycled materials and being maintenance-free; no paint or stain necessary. Several companies make kits that make the plastic beds even easier to build, with pieces that snap together.

Timbers as raised bed

If constructing beds out of wood, try to use boards that are at least two inches thick and six inches wide. Cut the boards to the length and width desired. Keep in mind that the beds should not be wider than four feet for ease of reaching across to weed. Build a frame using four-by-four-inch posts at the four corners and screw the boards into the posts, again making certain the boards are level and square.

Raised beds do not have to be more than about two feet high, enough to add at least 12 to 18 inches of good soil and compost. But if you prefer a higher bed of 18 to 24 inches so you can sit on the edge, make sure the construction is sturdy enough to support the weight of a person sitting and leaning on the sides. You may want to add a small ledge to the top of the sides for a more comfortable seat. Stake these frames into the ground for security while sitting. Depending on the construction materials and the length of the sides of the bed, you may also want to stake it into the ground halfway along each side so that the frame is stable when filled with soil and compost.

Most raised beds are placed directly onto the ground, but you can line the bottom with layers of newspaper or cardboard to discourage weeds from coming up through the soil. If you are plagued with bur-rowing creatures such as voles or moles, staple hardware cloth or screen-

Anchoring a raised bed into the ground with stakes

Coastal Gardening in the Pacific Northwest

ing to the bottom of the frame before you place it on the ground. And if you are handy with construction skills, you may want to add a hinged glass top to the frame to turn it into a cold frame, allowing an even earlier planting of seeds or vegetables. Recycling old lumber and windows makes this an even easier and lower-cost project.

A completely organic method of building raised beds is to use a frame of chicken wire, supported with 36-inch stakes driven into the ground at the corners and at several places along the sides. Use bales of hay, flaked, to line inside the wire fence. When the hay is baled, the layers will easily peel apart into flakes. These flakes will keep the soil from falling through the chicken wire. It will also prevent seeds from germinating along the sides of the raised bed. The hay will gradually decompose, enriching the soil. Place leaves, grass clippings, or decomposing, seedless weeds in the bottom of the bed. A 10- or 12-inch layer of good soil goes on top of the base and a final six-inch layer of compost is placed on the top of the soil.

If creating the beds in the fall, you can use mildly aged compost as the bottom layer. As the compost ages, it will not only be good for raising the soil level but will also give off heat in the decomposing process. To get more volume, alfalfa can also be used as a filler on the bottom of the beds. The alfalfa has no seeds and will break down, acting as fertilizer.

If you are planting vegetables in your raised beds, be sure and rotate the family of crops each year to keep pests and diseases from coming back to the beds. This is good advice whether using raised beds or not. Raised beds allow for more compact and intensive plantings each year as well.

Amendments

If you do not have a compost pile on the property, look into various ways of hauling compost in. Local garden centers will have bagged or loose compost available or know where you may find it in your area. Some areas in British Columbia have companies available that use kelp, seaweed, or fish "manure" as compostable material, called "Sea Soil." Agricultural areas with beef or dairy cattle may have composted steer manure available for purchase. Tillamook County, Oregon, has a digester plant where waste products from the dairy cows are processed and aged to make a wonderful organic amendment. Its high pH helps to counteract the acidic soils found on the coast. Clean, aged horse manure with no bedding materials in it is also good for plants. Avoid using pig or chicken manures, however, as they may contain harmful pathogens and bacteria. Do not use fresh manure on a garden, either. It will burn new plants. Instead, whatever type of manure you are using, make sure it has aged at least 10 months and till it thoroughly into the soil. This is best done for a vegetable bed in the autumn of the year in order that the manure has time to further age and mellow before spring planting.

DUNE PLANTINGS

Most plants do not do well in sandy soil because of the inability for the sand to hold water and release nutrients. Sand doesn't mean you can't grow anything in it. But it does mean more frequent watering and fertilizing, neither of which is desirable in an easily sustainable garden. Many plants cannot handle the salt sprays or the strong winds that are experienced along the ocean beaches. A simple walk along a dune area of the Pacific Coast will present ideas for plants that will not only survive, but thrive. The trick is to plant them in a way that will create a true garden and not just an "organized dune." You may want to consider using native plants in more creative ways. Just because you are using native plants doesn't mean your garden has to look like a natural sand dune if you prefer a more groomed or formal look to your garden.

There are two opposing positions of the garden design spectrum: the formal and the informal. Style-wise, the Japanese garden could be considered formal while the classic cottage garden is considered informal. And there are many stages between the two. Both can be very successful in the sandy soils along the ocean—it is a matter of design elements and choice of plants.

Japanese Gardens

Some of the best-planned gardens I have seen in the dune areas are ones that emulate the Japanese garden. There are garden purists who say that the only true Japanese garden is one that is located in Japan. And there are many garden designers that feel Japanese gardens do not have a place in America. In the strict sense, this is true. Japanese gardens are in Japan. So for the sake of discussion, let us only say that we are more interested in the elements of a Japanese-style garden.

One of the easiest ways to decide if this type of garden may be something you would like to try in your own yard is to visit one of the Japanese-style gardens that dot the Pacific Northwest. It is widely known that the Japanese garden in Washington Park, west of the city of Portland, Oregon, not only has wonderful views of Mount Hood, but also is one of the best Japanese gardens outside of Japan, albeit there are others older and more frequently visited. The view of Mount Hood is

reminiscent of Mount Fuji, with its snow-covered peak, and gives a feeling of authenticity to the garden itself. A visit is an excellent way to spend an afternoon even if you aren't interested in a Japanese garden for your own yard. And there are many ideas to be found there that can be easily adapted to a coastal garden. There are several other excellent examples of Japanese-style gardens in the Pacific Northwest and you will find a list of them in the "travel" section of this book.

There are also several magazines and books that are dedicated to the Japanese style of gardening. There is no harm in using them for inspiration, but try not to copy them plant for plant or stone for stone. Beside the fact that this may be difficult to achieve, we want this to be your design and you will need to take into account your plant preferences, your property size, and its shape and slope. There are many coastal plants that will fit into the Japanese design, and you should explore which of these appeal to you. Make a list of your favorites on a separate sheet so you can plot where they might work in your garden.

Before we continue, once again we must return to the concept of fitting the garden to the home and its surroundings. A Japanese-style garden will look best with a simply designed home with clean, horizontal lines, perhaps only one story tall. If your home is a more traditional beach cottage-style house, this may not be the garden for you. We will discuss other possibilities later.

When I suggest trying a Japanese garden for your dune home, many people will get the idea they need to hire a professional designer to come and create a garden for them. And if you want as authentic a Japanese garden as is possible in the Pacific Northwest, you may find a professional to be well worth their fees. A true Japanese garden has plants placed in certain ways, using triads to symbolize "Earth, Man, and the Heavens" or "Environment, Intellectuality, and Spirituality." Rocks and stones are very important and the way they are placed in the garden is more important still. Japanese garden designers have been known to place only the stones in the places desired and walk away from the project, leaving their garden workers to install the plants.

But although we don't have to plan a traditional Japanese garden, we can adapt some of its design elements to our dune garden. And if we call it a meditation garden instead, it will suggest we do not have to stick quite so closely to the rules of Japanese gardening. We can have our own interpretations.

How easy is this? A Japanese-style meditation garden employs the use of water, rocks, and sand. We already have the water and the sand, now all we have to do is minimize the rest of the area and place a few plants to create a meditative space we can enjoy. And because the number and size of plants is limited in a meditation garden, it can be low maintenance as well. There are several tenets we will still try to adhere to while designing our meditation garden. For example, we will stress not only simplicity but functionality. To be functional, we will want to think of the use of the garden. Will it be for play or entertaining or meditation? Or will it simply be a visual delight? You may choose to have only three or five different kinds of plants.

Tone of the garden is also important, whether it be formal or informal. Japanese gardens are generally very carefully tended and groomed, just at different levels. The tone of the garden will largely depend on how much time you have to spend on the maintenance. A true Japanese garden does not mix the tones. It is sometimes acceptable to add a touch of semiformality to either the formal or informal. But too much mixing of tones will cause disharmony in the garden, something we will try to avoid.

There are also variations on the Japanese theme. One that would be well adapted as dune gardens is the style called *Karesansui* or "dry garden." This garden has very little plant matter, relying on sand and stones for decorative elements. The sand represents flowing water while

Festuca glauca
'Elijah Blue' (Blue
fescue) and
Phormium (New
Zealand flax)

the rocks represent mountains. To be most successful, choose large rocks that have character and are well sculpted by the elements. Of course you may add as many plants as you feel comfortable with since this is your garden.

Keep in mind that our meditation garden should be a place to connect with nature, using all of our five senses—touch, smell, sight, hearing, and taste—plus the realms of time and balance. We will try to address all four seasons. We want to celebrate nature with more than plants; we want to use wood, stone, or water. We need to address our specific locality in our design and make it indicative of the Pacific Northwest, perhaps by using native wood, stone, and plants.

Our goal is a peaceful, soothing respite where we can feel comfort and protection.

The easiest way to begin is to start your plan from inside the house, using the architectural features to guide your eye. What will you want to see as you look out your windows and doors? Does your patio or deck lend itself to a simple garden? This is where the graphs of your yard and photographs of your home will come in handy.

PLANT CHOICES

One of the most important factors in creating a garden at the coast is being able to choose plants that will do well there. Of course, this is a critical element in any garden, but especially at the coast. The style of a garden may change over time, but the plant matter used will make or break the garden's success. By carefully selecting plants that will do well in a dune area and yet fit the simple designs of a Japanese-style garden, we will increase our chances of achieving a pleasing design.

Start first with the "bones" of the garden. The term bones has become a staple in the vocabulary of landscape designers and it basically means the large trees and shrubs that will give a garden its shape and

Thuja orientalis **'Golden Thread' (dwarf)**

Coastal Gardening in the Pacific Northwest

mark its boundaries. Some of the most traditional trees for a Japanese-style garden are of course, Japanese maples (*Acer palmatum*). There are many colors, shapes, and sizes ranging from coral bark maples like 'Sango Kaku' or the small, weeping 'Crimson Queen'. An added benefit to having these small maples in your garden is the variety of fall color they can bring. They also have a nice shape to their limbs, giving them winter interest after their foliage has dropped. There is a leaf shape and color to suit every need. The *Acer palmatums* seem to do well at the coast as long as they have some shelter from the winds. They are not a fussy tree and require only a reasonably steady supply of water in well-drained soils. Some will not tolerate salt buildup in the soil and will reflect this by a burned look to the edges of its leaves. This can be corrected by a

Using variegation
instead of flowers
for interest

regular leaching of the soil around the tree's roots, flooding it with tap water and letting the water drain slowly, taking the salt with it.

There are many small shrubs that will serve well in a meditation garden. Azaleas, *Pieris japonica*, hebes, and even boxwood can be used. Choose dwarf varieties if your garden is a smaller one. Most Japanese gardens rely on different foliage shapes for interest rather than color in flowers, with the exception of spring-blooming azaleas and cherry trees. There are many variegated shrubs being bred that will give year-round interest without bloom.

An excellent plant for a Japanese-style dune area would be one of the native beach grasses. Beware of using the European beach grass (*Ammophila arenaria*), however, as it has escaped cultivated gardens and is crowding out the native grasses on the dunes. This is a hint of how aggressive it can be. It is a lovely grass, however, and if you like the look, consider planting clumps in large pots, sunk into the ground. Pots are an excellent way of not only containing the grass in its desired area, but having more control over soil content as well.

Preferable is the North American native dune grass (*Elymus mollis*). Look for local nurseries that carry native plants or find them online.

European Beach
Grass
(*Ammophila
arenaria*)

Coastal Gardening in the Pacific Northwest

Please be a responsible gardener and do not consider digging the native beach grasses from a natural area, as this will negatively affect the dune areas. This is true even if you own the land on which the native grasses already grow. These natives are difficult to find in the wild anyway because of the encroachment of the European beach grass, so purchase indigenous plants from a reputable grower instead.

Elymus mollis (Native beach grass)

Native beach grass of course does well in the sand and still manages to give a Japanese feel to the garden, but other grasses also do well in sandy areas. Try *Imperata cylindrica* 'Rubra Red Baron' (Japanese bloodgrass). *Poa macrantha*, the seashore bluegrass, is also nice and native to the dunes of Washington, Oregon, and northern California.

Another lovely native grass is slough sedge (*Carex obnupta*). It prefers wetter conditions than most dunes can provide, but I find it does very well in my drier sandy soil. It also has an almost black inflorescence, which makes it very dramatic in a large grouping.

For a smaller groundcover grass, one of my favorites is large-headed sedge (*Carex macrocephala*). This one has stems about two inches tall with a large, dense inflorescence. Large-headed sedge is not comfortable to walk on, so its perfect for areas where you desire no foot traffic.

There are several other dune plants that will give some color to your garden. Tree lupines (*Lupinus arboreus*) are an evergreen shrub that may get to be quite tall, ranging from two to nine feet high and wide. Most bloom yellow but occasionally can be found in blue or violet. The cone-like racemes are sweetly scented, and it flowers from March through June. Naturally found in canyons and sandy areas in Northern California, it was also introduced as a sand binder in Oregon and Washington. They prefer poor soil and grow rapidly. Because of its deep roots, this is an excellent plant for stabilizing coastal dunes.

Carex obnupta
(Slough sedge)

Yellow sand verbena (*Abronia latifolia*) is a creeping plant about six inches high that is a good choice for dune areas. It flowers May through August and is native to the Pacific coastal areas from Southern California to British Columbia. It is the only known yellow sand verbena. *Abronia umbellata*, the pink sand verbena, has flowers that range from white to deep pink. Menzies' wallflower (*Erysimum menziesii*) is also a short plant good for dune areas. It blooms from March until May and will form low, conical mounds of solid yellow flowers when in full bloom. Seaside daisy (*Erigeron glaucus*) is another yellow creeper that is found from Southern Oregon to Southern California. This daisy's blooms range in color from white to a light purple.

Coastal Gardening in the Pacific Northwest

Carex macrocephala (Large-headed sedge)

Powdery dudleya (*Dudleya farinosa*) has the same range from Southern Oregon to Baja California. But this little plant is more akin to the sedum family with whitish stalks and clusters of yellow flowers that grow from rosettes. It has the appearance of being coated in a whitish powder, hence its name. It is also known as cliff lettuce.

Pretty as these dune plants are, they are basically wildflowers and should not be removed from the wild. Collecting seeds is the best way to propagate for your own gardens.

DESIGNING YOUR GARDEN

After compiling a list of possible plants, being certain to make note of their mature size, you can start to plot them onto your graph. This is more fun if you make scale-sized circular or free-form cutouts. Color the plant cutouts green or use green-colored paper and label them by species. Cut out separate circles for stones and color them gray or brown. Move the cutouts around on your garden graph until you are pleased with the symmetry and balance. You may then outline them in pencil onto the graph. Pencil is best because you may still want to make changes. If you prefer, you may want to lightly tape them down instead. Set your plans aside for a day or two while you call the utility company. When you return to them, you will have a fresh eye and may want to make a few more adjustments. Better to be patient at this stage than try to physically move the plants later.

Once you are satisfied with the paper plans, you can move to the yard and transfer your design to the lawn. If you have curves in your design, you may want to use a garden or soaker hose to lay along the perimeter. Rope or twine can also be used but they tend to lie in more severe lines and not in the gentle curves of the hoses, and they are more easily tangled or shifted. Using carpenter's chalk, mark the lines on the lawn, following closely to the hoses. Once you have marked along the hose line with your chalk—and called the utility company—you are ready to continue.

Remove any plants in the area that will not stay in the design. If you are using them in the meditation garden (or in other areas of your yard), place them into appropriate sized pots in a different "holding area" with conditions similar to the ones they just left. For example, if they were in the shade, place them somewhere else shady. Be sure to re-plant them to the level they were when they were removed. Water them well. By potting them it will make it easier to place them in the garden later. Even if you are not using them again, consider placing them in pots to be given to friends for their gardens.

Dig the area to about four inches deep, removing the grass and its roots and any other plants such as weeds or undesirables. A careful and thorough cleaning of the area at this stage will decrease the chance of encroaching weeds in the future. Now you may set out the pots of any plants you have chosen to complement your garden. This can include the ones you are reusing or plants purchased for this space. Set them out according to your design plan, but move them around until you have found an arrangement that is balanced and pleasing to your eye. Be sure not to use too many plants. This is not the full, crowded look of a cottage garden. You are striving for simplicity, the basis of Japanese design.

Dig holes for the plants that are about twice the diameter of the pots they are in and the same depth. If you need to amend each hole, this is the time to do so. Place water in the hole to about one-quarter the depth and wait for it to soak the soil. Remove the plant from its plastic container by lightly pressing on the sides of the pot. Loosen the roots gently. This is especially important if the plant is pot-bound. You may have to cut into some of the roots to keep them from encircling the root ball. Place the plant in the prepared hole at the same height as it was in the pot and backfill with soil. Firmly press around the sides of the plant to eliminate air pockets and give the roots firm contact with the soil. Water again thoroughly.

Once the plants are in place, lay down small rocks or gravel to the first two—or a little more—inches of depth. This is to make it hard on any weeds or grasses to come up through the gravel.

Now you can lay your larger stones. How large depends on the ultimate size of the garden. Boulder-sized rocks will look nice in a larger garden. If your garden is small, you may still want a single very large rock and a series of smaller ones. Don't place too many rocks in the area. Once again, you want to avoid a crowded look. Choose rocks of the same or contrasting color tones, depending on your personal preference. You may want a white stone base with black stones placed in patterns of waves or circles. If you are patient and creative, use black stones to create Japanese or Chinese characters in the gravel as well. Smooth river rocks are ideal and lend a more soothing look than the sharp edges of gravels. Your imagination is the only limitation of design patterns. You may also like the look of a sand area that is raked into patterns that make it resemble the ripples in a stream. This presents more maintenance problems as the sand may need to be raked often, especially if you live where the wind will undo your carefully tended patterns. However, raking the sand once or twice a day may be a form of mediation in itself, and if a Japanese-style mediation garden appeals to you, go for it!

GARDEN ALTERNATIVES

Not everyone will appreciate the stark, simple style of a meditation garden. There are other alternatives, one of which is the cottage-style garden that we will discuss in a later chapter. A very nice garden can be created at the shore by using only grasses, sedges and rushes. This type of all-grasses garden has been popularized in the prairies of the central United States and Canada. But they can also be translated into lovely gardens at the shore by using proper plant selections.

There are already native grasses that we know will grow well at the beach: Slough sedge, native beach grass, large-headed sedge and blue

wildrye. In fact, some of them grow so well as to become invasive. So careful planning is called for when using the creeping type of grasses. By planting in segregated areas or even raised beds, we can eliminate some of the tendency of these grasses to escape domestication.

An attractive grouping of grasses

The following list details some further suggested plants that can tolerate wind and salt-laden air near the coastal areas.

Trees

Juniperus virginiana (**eastern red cedar**): 40–50 feet high, 15–30 feet spread.

Pinus thunbergii (**Japanese black pine**): Fast growing in PNW to 100 feet high and 40 feet wide. Can be pruned as a cascade or as a large bonsai or sheared top for Christmas tree. Spreading branches with age.

Pinus mugo mugo (**mugho pine**): Slow growing to 4–8 feet high and 8–15 feet wide. Shrubby, symmetrical pine that may spread as it ages.

Quercus ilex (**holly oak**): Evergreen growing 30–60 feet tall and wide. Will grow in constant sea wind but may stay shrubby in such a location.

Shrubs

Agave americana (**American century plant**): Warmer zones, large, 10-foot spread. Difficult to move once established due to spines and bulk.

Baccharis pilularis (**dwarf coyote brush**): 8–24 inches high, spread to 6 feet or more. Native to Northern California coast, good bank cover, low maintenance.

Escallonia **spp.**: Zones 5–9, depending on species; larger shrubs, can be pruned to more manageable sizes. Tolerates wind and salt but damaged by high alkalinity, so acid soil is a must to reach full growth potential.

Genista pilosa 'Vancouver Gold' (**broom**): This broom is not the invasive one we see in roadside areas. It is a small (1–2 feet), deciduous shrub with a prostrate growing habit that can spread to 7 feet. Blooming May to June with small yellow flowers. It does need good drainage but poor, sandy soils are fine.

Ilex vomitoria (**yaupon**): Evergreen 15–20 feet tall and 10–15 feet wide. Takes extremely alkaline soils better than most hollies. Good topiary or trained into columnar forms.

Juniperus conferta (**shore juniper**): 1 foot tall, 6–8 foot spread. Good ground cover.

Pittosporum tobira (**tobira**): Japanese shrub with dense growth 6–15 feet high and wide. Can be headed back or pruned but not sheared. Good hedge or screen plant. Best in Zones 9 and up, but may be worth trying in cooler zones.

Prunus laurocerasus (**English laurel**): This can get to be quite a large shrub (15–30 feet high) and acts as an excellent screen from the winds. They don't seem to mind the salt spray. But they are also fast growing and so probably not good for a more formal hedge as they would need pruning often during the growing season. Instead, try a dwarf variety 'Otto Luyken', which has a nice, short form 3 to 4 feet high and 5 to 6 feet wide. It has very dark green leaves and pretty white flowers.

Viburnum, skimmia, and daphnes also do well in sheltered coastal gardens.

Perennials

(Most Japanese-style gardens rely on variegation and blooming shrubs and trees for interest, so the colorful and constantly blooming annuals are rarely used.)

Prunus laurocerasus 'Otto Luyken' (Laurel 'Otto Luyken')

Coastal Gardening in the Pacific Northwest

Euphorbia characias (**perennial spurges**): Mediterranean natives, can be 4 feet high and wide; drought resistant and prefer full sun.

Phlox drummondii (**annual phlox**): 6–18 inches high and 10–12 inches wide. Plant in spring in cold winter climates and fall with mild winters. Rich soil with organic matter and full sun.

Portulaca oleracea (**purslane**): Edible "weed" but tolerates most soils and wind. Low growing to 6 inches high and 1.5 feet wide. Easy to control if pulled before going to seed.

Gunnera tinctoria (**dinosaur food**): This is a huge perennial and so needs lots of space in the garden. It needs part shade and lots of water. It also likes nutrient-rich soil, so will need to be fertilized three or more times a year. Since it is from South America, it is a tropical-looking plant, but it cannot take the strong drying winds, so tuck it under some tall trees for protection from the salt spray.

Grasses

Muhlenbergia capillaris (**pink muhly grass**): Mounded grass, 3 feet high and wide. Drought tolerant but best with some water; evergreen in mild winters, tan or brown with hard freezes. Full sun or light shade.

Euphorbia characias wulfenii

Panicum virgatum: 2- to 4-foot-wide clump with airy clouds of white to pink inflorescences. Foliage and flowers persist all winter as beige colored.

Gunnera tinctoria

Cyperus alternifolius (**umbrella grass**): This member of the sedge family likes rich, moist soil and can even grow in water (but not salt water), so it makes a good pond plant. Remove any brown or broken stems. This plant is easily divided by removing the older center and saving the outer growth to replant. A dramatic plant, *Cyperus* resembles papyrus, giving a tropical look to the garden. One of those rare plants that actually prefers wet feet.

THREE

COASTAL MOUNTAIN GARDENING

MOUNTAINS

SHOULD YOU BE FORTUNATE enough to have lived near or visited the Pacific Northwest coast for more than a few hours, you will realize pretty quickly that not all coastal gardening is created equal. The warming effect of the ocean gives us the gardening possibilities of the United Kingdom. The zones are similar and the plant possibilities are reminiscent of the typical English coastal gardens. However, there is a major difference: mountains.

The Oregon, Washington, British Columbia, and Northern California coasts are blessed with the dramatic coastal mountain ranges that in some cases drop to the sea in spectacular views. We can watch the ocean from several vantage points, ranging in height from sea level to 1,000 feet above. The coves and capes present the traveler with varied and interesting scenes as Route 101 weaves its way north and south. This also makes gardening taxing.

To have a successful garden in the mountains, you must first take into account proximity to the ocean. The closer the garden is to the Pacific, the more sandy the soil will be. The further inland and the higher the elevation, the soil will become composed more of clay and rock. This doesn't mean you have to give up on a garden, just be aware of design elements such as terracing, raised beds, and wind breaks.

Mountain gardens will have wind almost as often as dune gardens have sea breezes. In fact, the coast ranges can have even more severe winds that whip through canyons, which act as wind tunnels. The difference is that the wind will not be as salt-laden as the oceanic winds. But they generally will be colder.

Another consideration with a mountain garden is the elevation. Gardens along the coast can be in Zone 8 or even a warmer Zone 9. But the higher the elevation, the lower the zone and the more limited you will be in your choice of plants. Elevation will also affect the amount of sun your garden will get in a day. You may be on a high plain where the full sun will allow a wonderful vegetable garden or even roses. Or you may be in one of those canyons where the sun doesn't peak the crest of the mountains until midday. This will also affect your choice of plants. One of my clients has a front garden that is in shade until mid-afternoon for about an hour and then is shaded again by the house in the late afternoon. We have chosen shade perennials and shrubs for the front of the house and full sun plants for the back that faces west.

Elevation will be a real factor during the changing seasons. As I mentioned before, when I moved into my coastal home in October, I was convinced I had a shade garden. I was busy planning what perennials I would buy in the spring to supplement what was already here. I followed my own advice—for a change—and waited a year to see what would crop up in the garden. It was a good thing I did. By mid-June I had full sun for most of the day. The sun was often very intense even though the air remained cool, and would have withered the hosta and brunnera I had planned on buying. The sun moves so much further north in the summer that the mountain that had blocked the light all winter was no longer a factor.

The amount of rainfall will also dictate your plant needs. The windward side will naturally have more rain; the leeward side less so. Irrigation may become a problem for those gardeners far from a spring or well. Time to consider drip irrigation or Mediterranean plants that need less water.

MEDITERRANEAN GARDENS

There is a relatively new term cropping up in gardening books and magazines called xeriscaping. The word is derived from the Greek *xeri* meaning "dry" or "needing little water." And this is basically what a Mediterranean Garden is: a garden that needs little summer water to survive and be healthy.

So we can take a lesson from the lush but drought-resistant gardens of Italy, Greece, southern Spain, and southern France as perfect solutions for coastal mountain gardens. We should take a moment to explore the topography and type of plants of the Mediterranean coast. Once again we encounter the purists who will say a Mediterranean garden can only be along the Mediterranean Sea. True. So let's call ours a Mediterranean-style garden.

First of all, we should define a Mediterranean region: mild, wet winters, mostly with rain instead of snow. Dry but warm summers. This includes all the countries that border the Mediterranean Sea, but also much of the West Coast of the United States, from Baja, Mexico, to the Washington coast and parts of Vancouver Island and British Columbia. Of course, the term "warm" will depend on latitude. The term "warm" in Mexico will certainly reflect higher temperatures than "warm" in Oregon. For our purposes, we will consider the Mediterranean climate to be about 55 to 75 degrees. Winters are also mild, having normal low temperatures about 30 to 50 degrees. This again spans from south of San Francisco to Vancouver Island. Temperatures are not as important to defining a Mediterranean-style garden as is amount and timing of rainfall.

True Mediterranean gardens are often divided into two or even three areas: a "hot" zone where gravel, sand, stone, and other hardscape plays an important role. This is generally a full-sun area. Here the plants take a reduced role in the landscape, although specimen plants are often highlighted with the gravel or stone or incorporated into stone terraces. Grass lawns are replaced by the gravel, stone, or sand areas, which act as places for our eyes to rest, just as turf does. Pebble or stone is also much more eco-friendly than lawns, as it does not require the vast amounts of water to keep it green and lush.

A xeriscaped walk in a Mediterranean garden

The second area is the "dry" zone, where drought-tolerant plants are located. These gardens are generally planted with perennials, grasses, shrubs, and trees that give year-long interest to the garden.

Lavendula stoechas (Spanish lavender)

The third, though optional, area is the "inner courtyard" type of garden where lush plants and water features give a sense of serenity and calm. These plants include the palms, bananas, and other tropical vegetation that like hot weather but need water as well. This area needs to be protected from salt-laden ocean winds or cold mountain winds, so if you don't have the trees, hedges, fences, or walls to accomplish this, this portion of a typical Mediterranean garden can be omitted.

The colors of a typical garden in the Mediterranean are cool blues, lavenders, turquoises, and silver, interspersed with the corals and salmons for interest and contrast. The color of terra cotta is used not only for pots but also for architectural hardscape such as patios and fountains. These color combinations can be very soothing.

Specific Mediterranean plants that do well in the coast ranges will depend on elevation, as we discussed earlier. But there are many plants that are hardy in colder temperatures and will also do well in climates with milder winters. The lavenders, several varieties of Cistus rockroses, and rosemary are good choices for a mountainous but coastal garden.

Spanish lavenders are good for informal as well as formal plantings and bloom most of the summer. All these plants prefer poor but well-drained soils, and will generally tolerate winds and salt better than more delicate plants. Once established, they also don't need much watering in the summer if they get sufficient rain in the winter months, definitive of the Mediterranean plants.

Crocosmia 'Lucifer'

More plants that like a dry summer but wet and mild winter are the hardier aloes and agaves, manzanita, ceanothus, crocosmia, euphorbia, and *Stipa gigantea* (giant feather grass).

Some plants will like a hot, dry summer but not much winter rain. Echinacea, liatris, penstemon, agastache, and coreopsis are all drought-tolerant if you can assure them of good drainage during the winter months. Rudbeckia love the full sun and well-drained soil of a Mediterranean garden.

If you do have a protected area and would like to try a courtyard with some lush tropicals, acanthus, agapanthus, canna lilies, dahlias, bananas, phormium, and passiflora might be worth trying. Be aware that some of these need winter protection and might best be grown in pots so they can be more easily moved indoors for the winter. And they all need good drainage.

Many bulbs are also suited for Mediterranean gardens. Bulbs can tolerate drought because they absorb nutrients in the spring and early summer and go dormant during the heat of the summer. Tulips, daffodils, crocus, ranunculus, anemone, muscari, and scilla are all excellent choices for naturalizing in a Mediterranean spring garden. They do need good drainage from the winter rains, however, or they will rot. This can be accomplished by amending the soil with sand or adding gravel underneath the soil when you plant the bulbs. You may also want to plant them in plastic mesh baskets. These can be easily sunk into the ground and disguised with mulch. The baskets can be then lifted in the fall and refrigerated at about 40 degrees for winter. The mesh baskets also help protect the bulbs from damage by rodents when food is scarce.

When considering a Mediterranean-style coastal garden be aware of certain four-legged problems: elk and deer. If you live in a wooded area, choice of plants becomes more important. Elk are more problematic than deer as they graze in large herds and will eat almost anything. They are much larger and more voracious eaters than the deer and can thus be very destructive to a newly planted garden. The best deterrent to elk, however, is at least an eight-foot-tall, sturdy fence or wall. Walls can at

Echinacea purpurea (**Purple Coneflower**)

least be made to look like stucco if you are trying for the Mediterranean look. Fences are a bit more difficult to disguise.

Rudbeckia (Brown-eyed Susan)

Deer are more particular about what they will eat, and there are lists of deer-resistant plants. However, deer do not usually read the lists and will try anything new in the garden just to test it. They may not like it and leave it alone, or they may develop a taste for it and eat it to the ground. They do generally leave herbs and grasses alone. Fortunately, many of the Mediterranean plants are herbs, so a large lavender bed with rosemary accents and a thyme border may be just the thing to keep the deer at bay.

You do not have to be totally authentic to Greece or Spain in your plant selection to have a Mediterranean-style garden—West Coast native plants can also be incorporated. The natives have adapted to the drier summers and wetter winters, or they wouldn't have lasted long enough to be called natives. Red- or yellow-twigged dogwoods (*Cornus stolonifera*) are excellent examples of native shrubs that give winter interest and do well in coastal areas. For a native tree that is indicative of a Mediterranean area, try a Garry Oak (*Quercus garryana*), also known as the Oregon white oak. In large, rocky, windy areas, its gnarled

Cornus stolonifera
'Flaviramea'
(yellow-twigged
dogwood)

branches are reminiscent of the olive trees seen so frequently in Spain and Italy. The difference is the Garry oaks' height, which can reach 120 feet. It is slow growing, however, and can be long lived, up to 300 years.

Any new plant—even xeriscape plants—will need one to two years of watering before it can establish strong and deep roots to sustain itself through dry summers. Watering deeply and thoroughly but less often for the first few seasons will encourage the root growth they need. Winter and spring rains in the Pacific Northwest should be sufficient to keep the plants happy, but if there is a dry period during the winter, be sure to water deeply once a month.

Fertilizing is generally not necessary in the first season if the initial planting holes were properly prepared. Fertilize the following October instead with a high quality compost or organic fertilizer because the root growth cycle will be thriving at this point. Fertilize the following season as needed.

Group your plants according to their watering needs. Place the xeric plants in south- or west-facing areas where they can soak up the sun and enjoy the dry soils.

Plants that need more moisture belong on the north- or east-facing areas of the garden. Mulching these plants will help retain necessary moisture and reduce evaporation when rain soaks the soils. Remember to replace the mulch, even if using gravel, each year. Check in the spring and fall for a mulch level of about one to two inches for maximum effect.

LAVENDERS

There are many varieties of lavenders that work beautifully in a Mediterranean garden. The Spanish lavenders (*Lavendula stoechas*) are excellent choices. They have narrow gray-green leaves and bloom earlier than many of the English varieties. Botanists feel the lavenders originated in Arabia and moved along the Mediterranean Sea to Greece, Italy, and eventually to Spain and France. They were brought to North America by English settlers, though, as they have long been popular in English gardens.

The lavenders prefer full sun and well-drained soil. The best mulch to use is white rock, sand, or gravel, which will reflect the light and heat and encourage drainage, keeping the diseases to a minimum. Organic mulch isn't as effective as it tends to hold in the moisture and slows drainage. Lavenders may be damaged if the temperatures drop below 28 degrees, so plant them next to a light-colored wall for protection and additional winter warmth.

The lavenders will need a little more soil preparation than other Mediterranean plants. They don't mind poor soil but they do hate wet roots and heavy, packed clay soils, so a bit of coarse soil amendment in the planting hole will promote drainage. Plant on a slope or in a raised bed to further encourage drainage. After their second growing season, you can water less frequently but still deeply. Do not overwater established lavender or other xeriscape plants.

The use of fertilizer on lavender is not required and other than an occasional pruning and cutting of flowers, these are easily maintained plants. Prune to old, yellowing leaves after bloom, but avoid cutting into the woody growth that has no buds as the plant may not be able to regenerate growth. The plants will—over time—form a bare center of woody growth that can't be pruned into with any success. In this case, replacement of the plant is the best option. With careful pruning, this won't occur for eight to ten years.

Lavenders are the backbone of a good xeriscaped garden but try companion planting with agastache, salvias, penstemon, yarrow, or coreopsis for maximum bloom time. These perennials are generally hardy and enjoy the same watering conditions as the lavenders and so will be easily maintained in the same conditions. The color palette can be one of harmony or contrast, depending on your preference.

MORE PLANT CHOICES

Once again, choice of plants is crucial to any garden's success. This may seem like an obvious statement, and one I have mentioned before, but some gardeners purchase plants that are inappropriate for their setting and can only lead to garden failure and gardener frustration. Being an informed consumer is the best way to avoid disappointment. Yes, I would love to have a peony in my garden, but I realize they do not do well close to the salt and sand, and so I must resolve to enjoy them when I go visiting inland gardens.

There are many beautiful plants that will do well in a mountain coastal garden, and some of the best are the rhododendrons and azaleas that are native to North America. Azaleas are considered to be in the rhododendron family, and are generally grouped together for good, healthy growth.

There are also hundreds of cultivated varieties of rhododendrons and azaleas that have been developed and will thrive in the mountains. Try to provide them with some shade if possible, as these were originally forest plants and their blooms will last longer if not in full sun. Too much shade, however, will produce leggy, uneven growth and lesser blossoms. Try to find a happy medium with some filtered shade. Some rhododendrons are now bred to tolerate full sun and are considered to be heat resistant. This is something a coastal gardener need not generally be concerned with, as by nature the coast is a cooler summer environment than inland valleys. Rhododendrons and azaleas also need protection from strong winds, especially salt-laden ones, but this usually can be achieved with the fences, walls, trees or buildings that are providing the plants with filtered shade.

There are colors, sizes, and shapes of rhododendrons to fill any garden's needs and any gardener's desires. There are also deciduous azaleas that lend not only winter interest with their gnarled branches, but spring fragrance. Almost any color except black can be found to add spring color to your garden borders. After the blooms have faded, deadhead them carefully so as not to disturb growth of next year's buds, which are already forming. You can also allow the flowers to drop naturally. The shape of most rhododendrons and evergreen azaleas provide nice backgrounds for summer and fall blooming plants as well. Training a summer-blooming clematis into a rhododendron can increase interest as well.

If you can grow rhododendrons, you can also grow camellias. These lovely spring-flowering shrubs can also get quite large, so prune them on an annual basis to maintain a reasonable size. They come in many colors of flowers, but they all have shiny, dark green foliage that can be used as a nice filler leaf in arrangements.

The best way to find a reputable grower of these plants is to ask fellow gardeners what their experiences have been. Many nurseries on the coast will have nice selections of rhododendrons but be aware of a wide-spreading disease called Sudden Oak Death, which has affected some Northwest-grown rhododendrons. More on that in chapter 6, "Potential Problems."

Rhododendron mollis (deciduous Azalea)

RIVERS   Camellia

The coastal mountain rivers of the Pacific Northwest are among its
most beautiful and valuable resources. The American River in California; the five rivers that flow into the Tillamook Bay in Oregon (the
Trask, the Wilson, the Kilchis, the Tillamook, and the Miami Rivers);
and the Quinault River in Washington are all examples of mountain
creeks that become rivers as they approach the Pacific Ocean. But for
gardeners living in riparian areas—the green areas along rivers—there
are abundant challenges.

    Rivers can be blessings in a hot, dry summer, or Mother Nature's
worst enemy when the floods occur during the winter months. Rivers
deposit layers of silt on the shore banks, but those same rivers can rob
the nutrients from the soil as they flood. A river gardener should be
aware of the limitations of living along banks of the rivers that flood
every five to ten years. Even small rivers or streams are apt to escape
their banks on a regular basis.

    River and stream ecosystems are fragile at best and so river gardeners
should be especially aware of the danger in using pesticides or even fertilizers near water sources. We can plant along riparian areas, but we

must be conscious of what we plant having an effect on the streamside. For example, Japanese knotweed was imported many years ago to stave off erosion along streams and rivers in Oregon and Washington. Well-meaning planners thought this fast-growing, low-maintenance plant would be excellent in holding on to riverbanks. And it was. But it has now escaped the rivers and instead threatens to choke out native species. The same has happened with the Buddleia, or butterfly bush. The butterflies and hummingbirds love them, but the seeds are spread so easily by birds and the wind that Buddleia, too, are considered weeds. Major conservation projects throughout the Pacific Northwest are involved in eradicating both of these noxious weeds. Many communities have guidelines for planting along riparian areas, so it is best to check with wildlife sources, local water districts, or your extension agent before introducing a new plant to the streamside. This is a good way to avoid the mistake of planting what may several years later become a noxious weed.

The choice of permissible plants to use in a riparian setting is interesting as well. The rich loam soil along a stream or riverbed can be relocated by the floods we mentioned before. The neighbor downstream at the bend will no doubt benefit from your rich soil until the next high water, when his neighbor will benefit from the next high water. Trees along the banks oftentimes act as erosion control, and these are best left in place if at all possible. They will generally be the native Oregon ash or Red alders and will be better adapted for high- and low-water variations as well as the shade that comes with the taller trees in coastal mountain areas.

ADDITIONAL PLANT CHOICES FOR MEDITERRANEAN AND XERISCAPE GARDENS

Trees

Cedrus deodara (**Deodara cedar**): A very large, long-lived tree that can grow to 80 feet in height with a spread of 40 feet. It prefers the milder, humid areas of the Pacific Northwest and will grow 30 feet in only 10 years. It likes full sun and deep, well-drained soil, like the rest of the cedars. It is drought tolerant. 'Aurea' is a nice variety with golden branch tips and a dropping lead shoot.

Cupressus (**cypress**): These are lovely trees and do well near the ocean. *Cupressus sempervirens*, also known as Italian cypress, is one of the best for the coast. Its tall, columnar shape is a good border tree, and it has a slow growth habit of about 15 to 20 feet in 10 years. Drought tolerant once established, this tree comes in a blue-green color

('Glauca') as well as dark green ('Stricta'). Needs little pruning or other care.

Pinus contorta contorta (**shore pine**): This hardy tree can be seen along the coastal areas from California to British Columbia and is well known for its windblown look. Its rapid growth and tolerance to salt-laden winds make it a good choice for the coastal garden. It can be pruned to maintain a reasonable height.

Sequoiadendron giganticum (**giant redwood**): Of course a Northwest icon, the giant redwood trees are lovely but unless you have a very large yard with deep soil, they aren't practical in a home garden. Best left for a woodland area or as a tall border. It is a fast grower (three to five feet per year in its native habitat) but it is almost entirely pest free. Its foliage is very soft looking, and the trunk of a healthy tree is almost a straight line along its height. The main branches grow straight from the trunk but smaller branches may droop slightly from the main ones. They like full sun to light shade with regular watering until established. After about five years, they will be able to draw needed water from the fog.

Shrubs

Ceanothus (**California lilac**): There are several ceanothus good for coastal gardens. The first is a ground cover, *C. glorious* 'Point Reyes Ceanothus'. It likes full sun and will only get to 12 inches tall and 3 to 4 feet wide. *C. thyrsiforus* is known as the "blue blossom ceanothus" and will reach a height of 15 feet. This is an evergreen and likes a dry north-facing bank for well-drained soil. The ceanothus also prefer a lighter soil. Some varieties are salt-spray resistant and are good in exposed positions. They do generally only live for 5 to 10 years before needing to be replaced, however.

Perovskia (**Russian sage**): Prune hard in mid-spring. Prefers average to poor soil and not much water for best growth and deepest color. Plant with other heat-loving varieties of xeriscape plants.

Taxus (**yew**): This is one of the few conifers that doesn't produce cones but fruitlike cups with a single seed. The seeds and foliage are poisonous. Yews can be grown as trees or shrubs, depending on the variety and the gardener's needs. They are long-lived and make excellent hedges and screens as they take well to pruning and shearing. They like sun or shade, depending on the variety, and regular watering. They do have a variety of pests, however, like scales, spider mites, and vine weevils. Hose off the foliage every two to three weeks during hot, dry spells in the summer.

Hebe: This group of small evergreen shrubs has a wide variety of uses in any coastal garden. Hebes have flowers that bloom in the spring

but the foliage also has a nice form the rest of the year. These are mainly mounding shrubs, but some varieties will act as groundcovers while others take a more upright form.

Vaccinium ovatum (**evergreen honeysuckle**): This native shrub has adapted very well to the entire Pacific Northwest coastal area. The shrub makes a nice accent with interest year round and especially in the new growth, which comes in as a reddish orange color. An added benefit is the delicious berries.

Perennials

Achillea (**yarrow**): Liking full sun, this plant has many varieties that will bloom all summer and late into the fall. The leaves are a gray-green and most of the flowers are a flat-topped yellow cluster. Good cutting flowers for bouquets. They need little care, just deadheading and cutting back once blooming is done. Once established, they are drought tolerant. Divide the clumps once they get too large for their space. This will promote better blooming in following years.

Aconitum (**monkshood**): Aconitum are good substitutes for delphiniums in the shade as they are tall, spiked, and usually blue-flowered.

Vaccinium ovatum (native evergreen huckleberry)

Some varieties can reach two to four feet high and will bloom from late summer into fall. Aconitum will die back in the winter, so mark their locations. They do need some winter cold. Plant or divide in late fall or early spring for best results. All parts of this plant are poisonous, so wear gloves and long sleeves when working with them to prevent dermatitis. Keep children and pets from their area.

Coreopsis: These members of the aster family have the traditional daisylike flowers atop airy foliage. Some are annuals, some perennials, and they generally have bright yellow, orange, or burgundy flowers. Easily deadheaded by using hedge shears for longer blooming time. Plants will self-seed but are divided without difficulty. *Coreopsis grandiflora* may bloom itself into exhaustion and may sprawl in midsummer. Cut back the flowering stems to the basal leaves in late summer to stimulate new foliar growth.

Aster: This is a large family (over 600 species) of daisy-shaped plants that range in size from tall plants for use in the back of a border to small mounding ones that are best used in front. Most garden asters bloom in late summer to mid-fall and are a nice complement or substitute for fall-blooming chrysanthemums. Most flowers are in the blue to purple range, but there is also a nice native aster that is bright yellow.

Hemerocallis (**daylilies**): All forms of daylilies are good choices for a Mediterranean (or Japanese or even cottage-style) garden. They will take full sun along the coast and most any kind of soil. Well-drained is best, though, as their fleshy roots may rot if left in standing water. They do not like strong wind, so try to give them some protection. Deciduous daylilies will do better in a colder area because they need a colder winter for best bloom. Evergreen lilies will need a layer of mulch in a colder area. There are many varieties of daylilies in all colors and sizes. They are very persistent and mostly trouble free once established. Divide the clumps in early spring about every three to five years. Each bloom lasts one day but with frequent deadheading, especially for repeat bloomers, you may be able to extend the season. Best done by snapping the entire flower head off between forefinger and thumb. I make this part of my daily evening routine all summer.

Lonicera (**honeysuckle**): If you are going to get a honeysuckle to cover a fence or trellis or arbor, be sure to get a fragrant one. Known for their scent, this group of flowering vines makes a nice addition to any style of garden. There are many varieties, some are deciduous, some are evergreen, some are semi-evergreen. They will take full sun to part shade, depending on the variety, and like a well-drained soil. Thin after blooming. You can also cut old straggling vines to the ground in early spring before the new growth appears. A box honeysuckle (*L. nitida*) makes a nice evergreen shrub that tolerates salt-laden winds.

Clematis: There is a clematis vine for every gardener and every garden, but the *C. montana* and *C. armandii* do especially well on the coast. They like as much full sun as possible but mulch the roots because they like to stay cool, and protect the plant from strong winds. Clematis climb by throwing their little leaves over a support and wrapping around it, so for best results, provide something small for the leaves to drape around, for example, twine or wire. They can also be nicely trained into rhododendrons, roses, honeysuckles, and other shrubs. There are three types of clematis and they each require different pruning techniques at different times of the year. Check with the nursery for which type you are purchasing.

Euphorbia: The euphorbias are related to the weeds known as spurges but are the showier, larger cousins. Their bloom time generally

Here, a net is being used as a support for clematis

begins in the very early spring or even late winter and lasts all summer. Readily self-seeding, but deadheading before the flowers go to seed can take care of this problem. The taller varieties can be cut back with hedge shears to keep a nicely mounded shape. Euphorbias do emit a sticky, milky sap that can cause dermatitis, so I generally wear rubber gloves and long sleeves and long pants when cutting back this plant.

Iris: Many of the iris family do well on the coast. The bearded iris will also do well if given shelter from salt-laden winds, but I find them not to be as carefree as I would like, so I stick with the hardier, easier Siberian iris. The Siberians also are not as prone to iris borers and diseases that plague the bearded ones. They prefer full sun, and most any type of soil, but resent being divided, which are more good reasons to have them. If you must move them, do so in the fall so they have the winter to recover. You may still lose a season's bloom.

Kniphofia: Also called the red-hot poker plant, the *Kniphofia* hybrids are getting to be more than just red and orange. Many more pastel colors are being developed. The spires of flowers tower above tall, grasslike foliage when they bloom in late spring and summer, depending on the cultivar. They prefer well-drained soil and need to be moved after blooming so they can recuperate before winter. Cut off the old flower spikes to the ground when the blooms are done, but keep the leaves for the winter. I prefer to tie mine with twine to keep the winter rains from rotting the crowns. I then cut the leaves back in the early spring to about four or five inches from the ground, staying clear of the crown.

Liatris spicata: Also known as purple gay feather, this very pretty spiked perennial comes in other colors such as cream or dark violet. *Liatris* have the unique talent of blooming from the bottom up and if deadheaded, may give a repeat bloom in late summer. They like well-drained soil and are drought tolerant. You may need to divide them every five years or so if you find the clumps are getting too large and the flowers are blooming less.

Lithodora: Lithodoras are most noted in the spring when they bloom in blue profusion as they cascade over walls or trail along the ground. The gray-green foliage sprawls from a single plant and weeding is easily done by gently lifting the branches and pulling out the weeds from underneath. By cutting a little back each spring after blooming, you will expose the leaves to the sun and the plant will remain healthier having not died back in the center. A great coastal ground cover. Mine have a small amount of bloom almost all year long.

Stachys byzantina: The fluffy, white-gray foliage of lamb's ears are a staple in most cottage gardens as well as Mediterranean yards. This plant needs a well-drained bed and prefers full sun but will do well in part shade. In very rainy areas, the older foliage can turn almost mushy, but this is remedied by cutting off the older foliage. Opening up the center of the plant by cutting back this older foliage will allow more light, thus prevent the leaves from rotting. Avoid watering from overhead during the summer. The tall purple or pink flower spikes are best removed so the plant doesn't put too much energy in going to seed.

ADDITIONAL PLANT CHOICES FOR RIPARIAN MOUNTAINOUS AREAS

Most of the plants in the Mediterranean gardens will do well in a mountainous riparian area if you provide them with the good drainage that is crucial to their survival. They will also need as much sun as you can provide.

Other possibilities include the rushes and native shrubs such as salals, rhododendrons and azaleas. Acanthus, the native goat's beard (*Aruncus dioicus*), astilbe, umbrella plant (*Darmera peltatum*), Japanese iris, monarda, and Solomon's seal can all handle wetter sites.

Annuals with hot colors such as calendula, sunflowers, and zinnias may be suited for a Mediterranean garden, although they can not be considered for a xeriscape because of their need for water. Put them in the "inner courtyard" instead. The annual African daisies (*Arctotis* hybrids), strawflowers, and gaillardias will do better in a xeriscape.

FOUR

COASTAL COTTAGE GARDENS

W E SHOULD PROBABLY START this chapter by defining a cottage garden. Essentially, it is the typical British type of garden with lots of shrubs, perennials, annuals, bulbs, and even vegetables. They generally surrounded small cottages in the rural districts, hence the name. Cottage gardens have a long history, especially in England, where Gertrude Jekyll lifted them to a higher level of design in the late 1800s and early 1900s by recommending gardeners plant perennial borders in drifts of color. Miss Jekyll, however, was designing mostly for large manor houses with huge, expansive gardens. This is not generally practical here on the Pacific Northwest coast, as the spaces for gardens tend to be defined by the size of the yard and closer to the house than the English manor houses. But we can use some of her design principles to create our coastal cottage garden.

Today's English cottage gardens can be found in the front areas of small lots in London as easily as in the foothills of the Cotswold Mountains or the suburbs of Dublin or Edinburgh. Contemporary British cottage gardens have evolved to the point that they can even be simulated on rooftops of condominiums in huge cities.

American cottage gardens have a different concept, generally because our yards and gardens are much larger than in Britain. And, of course, by nature, Americans seem to generally prefer things bigger and brighter than our European cousins. We favor the new, the modern, and the unusual. Our gardens are no exception, and we strive to have unique and varied plants there too. But the basic premise is the same for an English or American cottage garden: lots of plants and lots of variety in those

A formal English
garden

plants. American cottage gardens are more likely to incorporate yard or
garden art, however, as well as more lawn than the British. Again, both
are indications of having more space to work with.

A fundamental rule to follow when planning a cottage garden in either a dune location or in the coastal mountains is to choose an area
with the best sun available, as most cottage garden plants prefer full to
part sun. Start small, even if you have a large area to cover with plants.
Try to do one area at a time, working in stages. A cottage garden can be
labor intensive at first, so by starting small you can always add more
garden if you find you have the time and energy. Creating too large a

Coastal Gardening in the Pacific Northwest

Gravel used as
path material

garden at the beginning will leave you frustrated and guilty that you
cannot spend enough time in maintenance. Put your paths in first, leaving lots of room for plants that won't impede the walkways. Any other
hardscape will be next: patios, walls, arbors, trellises, etc.

Ideally, you have started with the suggestions in chapter 1 and built
up your soil with amendments and organic matter. Any garden does
better with good soil, and the cottage garden is no exception. You will
need to continue to build up the soil as the garden ages, adding compost and mulch on a yearly basis, more often if necessary.

When you begin to plant your garden, the largest plants—trees and
shrubs—should usually be placed first. Next will come the plants and

bulbs of the perennial borders or islands. Finally will come the annuals, pots, and hanging baskets. As always, it is better to plan on paper first because of the simplicity of correcting mistakes before the holes are dug. Keep in mind the mature size in height and width of each plant and you will have less moving to do in the future. This is an easy concept to understand but a difficult one to execute, as we all want instant gratification of mounds and mounds of flowers. Toward this end we often plant our perennials too close together. My favorite perennial-related quote is "First year—sleeping; second year—creeping; third year—leaping." This is true of most perennials and in only three years they will fill out the space nicely.

If you do not have full sun in your garden, there is still a wide variety of shade-loving plants that will give a cottage feel. Heucheras, hostas, astilbes, and brunneras are hardy enough to be planted in mountain shade, and if you can amend sandy soil, they will do relatively well near the ocean. Provide them with some protection from salt-laden winds, and they will brighten a shady spot in your yard. Many of these plants will do well in part shade, too. Some even prefer a little morning sun but need protection from the intense afternoon sunlight.

The seemingly random and haphazard way of planting a cottage garden is actually an orchestrated maneuver. But by giving it a random feeling also makes it a bit easier to experiment with plant choices. If something doesn't work in a season or two, it can be moved to a more desirable area or removed all together. Try to repeat colors, forms, and foliage in a broad pattern to lend harmony to the flower beds and unite the garden.

A cottage garden is a more informal garden than most. The design and feel of a cottage garden should be welcoming. The look of chaos is misleading—these gardens are certainly planned. Exact plants may not appear on your graphed pages, but by titling general areas "blue and white perennial border" or "vine vegetables" or "red annuals" on your graph, it will lend itself to assigning specific plants at a later time. A conventional cottage garden usually has a wide variety of plant matter. By choosing plants that will work in your USDA Zone, you have the opportunity to create a cottage garden in the coastal mountains as well as on the dunes. Yet again, the choice of plants is critical to success, but hardscape is also an important part of the feel of a cottage garden. The hardscape may be similar at either a mountain or a shore location. Choose what you like, but remember moderation when it comes to type of materials and quantity of garden art and accoutrements.

COTTAGE HARDSCAPE

We refer to hardscape in a garden as generally being anything that isn't plant matter. Use of patios, arbors, walls, gates and fences, paths, trellises, and tunnels are characteristics of a cottage garden, and personal selections can make each garden unique. Proper location of garden art and sundials, armillary spheres, wells, or old-fashioned pumps can add a touch of whimsy or intrigue by luring the visitor farther down the path. Cottage gardens are often broken into "rooms," and each room may even have a separate use. The hardscape elements can help to create unity within these rooms and allow passage from one room to another. There is a fine line between good design and too much clutter, however, and not all of these design elements should be used at the same time unless your garden is quite large and can be broken into several separate areas.

Paths and Patios

Paths are traditionally made of brick, stone, or gravel. Newer materials such as pavers or interlocking cement blocks can also be used. The paths should be at least four feet wide to allow comfortable movement throughout the garden. Place these first so you can better define the planting beds.

Patios are also made of brick, stone, or pavers. Gravel is generally not used for a patio because you need something solid that will support the weight of a table or a few chairs. You can locate your patio in the sun or in the shade; each will have its own use. You may be lucky enough to have a yard large enough for a sun patio and a shade one.

Arbors, Arches, and Trellises

Arbors are nicest when planted with scented climbers such as honeysuckle, jasmine, or one of the fragrant clematis. Arbors, generally made of wood, metal, woven reeds, or even bamboo, can be against a wall or fence, with a bench underneath to act as a getaway place. Or they can be freestanding in the center of the garden to act as an entrance to a different part of the yard. If a freestanding arbor is your choice, make sure to anchor it well into the ground. Arches are similar to arbors but involve a passage through a wall or fence. These also can be made of brick or wood and again act as entryways.

Trellises are usually secured to a wall or fence as a support for climbing plants. Roses and clematis are examples that look nice climbing on a trellis. These can also be freestanding, but must again be secured so as not to fall in a wind or be accidentally knocked over. If securing to a

Pavers invite us
along a winding
path

wall, do so in a manner to allow air behind the trellis and perhaps have the trellis on hinges at the bottom in case it needs to be gently folded back to paint the wall or fence.

Garden Art

Garden art made from recycled materials, mosaics, hypertufa, ceramics, copper, or wood are becoming increasingly popular. You have the choice of creating something yourself or shopping at a local artist's studio. Often plant sales will include vendors who sell yard art. Yard sales, estate sales, and garage sales are also excellent places for inspiration.

Another piece of hardscape that is becoming popular are obelisks. These can be made of wood or metal in a three- or four-sided, free-standing design and are generally for the support of a climbing perennial, annual, or vegetable. Painted a bright color, they can also act as yard art and add height and whimsy to the garden.

Sundials give a nice touch to the cottage garden as do bird houses, bat houses, and butterfly houses. Armillary spheres, the metal astronomical devices that show a sphere within a sphere to represent the celestial heavens, can also be placed in a garden. Armillary spheres and sundials are best placed on some sort of plinth or stand as a focal point in an area.

Fences and Walls

Fences are also considered to be hardscape. They can be picket, which are commonly used to define a front garden, or post and rail, which are largely used for longer spans in a country setting. Solid wood fences are not recommended on the coast because of the wind. Staggered board fences that allow air movement to pass through are more desirable and if done properly, can offer the same privacy as a solid fence.

Walls in a cottage garden are traditionally made of dry-stacked stone. This allows extra protection for the plants and is a welcoming

A fence constructed out of bamboo

feature as well. Try, if possible, to use local stone. If a dry-stacked wall is to be higher than two or three feet, a knowledgeable stone mason is recommended to make the wall sturdy and secure. There are now also man-made landscape blocks that can be easily stacked to be a more uniform wall. These are formed to simulate a rough stone wall and since all the blocks are made to look alike, this type of wall will lend itself to a more formal look in the cottage garden. Local home-and-garden centers will generally carry these blocks and offer construction classes for the beginner.

THE NEXT STEP

It's easiest to go back to your yard graphs and place your plant cutouts on these graphs before you start to move the plants around. Again, label your cutouts with native plant names. Of course, you may also choose some nonnatives that are location specific as well. And you won't need cutouts to emulate stones as we did for the meditation garden in chapter 2, but you might want to use cutouts of benches, tables, and chairs instead.

Don't forget to call the utility company before you plan your garden so you can plot those utility lines on your planning graph. This should always be done before installing hardscape or digging for plants.

COTTAGE PLANTS

Once again we must return to soil type before we choose specific plants for our garden. This is when the pH can be crucial. Because of the normal acidity of rainfall (and I am not talking about "acid rain" here, which is a different thing altogether), and the decomposition of coniferous forests, the Pacific Northwest tends to have acidic soil. Thus, unless you have the time to amend the soil further to obtain a higher pH, the types of plants you choose should prefer acidic soils. The native plants are prime examples of acid lovers: rhododendrons, salals, shore pines, lupines, and native grasses.

If you already have some native plants in your garden, you may choose to either incorporate them in your design or move them. This, of course, will depend on the size of the plant and whether they are currently at a mature size. An established garden is harder to remove and you will have to be diligent at getting out *all* the roots of *all* the plants. Leaving even a bit of a root may give the plant enough energy to resprout, spoiling your carefully thought-out plan. It may be easier to leave large trees and shrubs in place, but if they really don't fit into your design, try to find them good homes. There will no doubt be people looking for mature plants for their own garden redesign so ask around to see if you can recycle these leftover plants. Contact local garden clubs or the county extension office and let them know you have plants to share. Placing them in pots until you are ready to replant them or passing them along to friends is a good idea that combines both sharing and recycling concepts. Plastic pots for transplants can often be found at recycling centers or in the potting sheds of most gardeners. I always save a few after a trip to the nursery for just this purpose.

As we briefly discussed earlier, a solid wood fence can sometimes create pockets of stronger wind force at its base as the wind passes over. The wind will slow as it passes through the branches of an evergreen hedge easier than it does through a fence. A hedge also lends a softer, more informal look to the garden. If a formal look is desired, however, hedges may be groomed by pruning them into rectangular or rounded shapes. This will have to be done twice each year, in the spring and fall, with a few touch-ups periodically to keep the hedge looking tidy. Some good choices for coastal hedges would be laurel, *Escallonia*, holly, *Taxus* (yew) and *Thuja occidentalis* (American arborvitae), all of which can grow to substantial size. For a shorter hedge, try *Buxus* (boxwood), cotoneaster, lavender, shrub roses, rosemary, or some varieties of *Lonicera*.

Using natives to set up a wind screen for the perennials that are less wind tolerant is a good idea as the natives are already adapted to the coastal conditions, either at the dunes or in the mountains. A hedge of salal, for example, would be a good choice to use as a wind block. *Escallonia* or laurel would also make good hedges and will grow taller than the salal. There is a very pretty plant called *Holodiscus discolor*, or ocean spray, that makes a beautiful, large, summer-blooming hedge. The large clusters of flowers are a creamy white and fade to a warm brown as they age. These can be left on for winter interest or pruned as they finish blooming.

Mixed borders can be nicely used in our American cottage gardens. This simply involves using ornamental grasses, small shrubs and trees, herbs, and annuals along with time-honored perennials. This type of mixed border is also typical of cottage-style gardens and would be a good choice for the mountainous areas along the coast. As we have already discussed, there are many natives to the coast that will do well in the mountainous areas as well as the dune areas. And nonnatives that are hardy to Zone 5 would also be good selections. But you need not limit yourself to native plants when creating an American cottage garden. The turf lily (*Liriope*) and coralbells (*Heuchera*) families of perennials do well in coastal exposures as does candytuft (*Iberis sempervirens*), fountain grass (*Pennisetum orientale*), *Kniphofia*, *Santolina*, and sedums and yuccas. A popular flower addition is the sea pink or thrift (*Armeria maritima*), which will bloom all summer long and will tolerate soil with a high sand content. This low-growing plant stays green all winter long as well.

Hydrangea species seem to thrive if given some wind shelter. They will bloom predominately blue because of the acidic soil, but many are now being bred that stay true to color regardless of the soil pH. Another good shrub choice for the warmer Zone 9 or above is the *Tibouchina urvilleana* (princess flower). This can get to be quite a large shrub but blooms with large deep-blue flowers in the autumn.

Herbs are excellent choices for a typical cottage garden and some are not only drought tolerant but enjoy full sun as well. The lavenders, rosemary, and thymes that we saw in the Mediterranean garden can also be planted in a more informal cottage garden with great success. They can be given their own corner of your garden or intermixed with other plants. Try to keep their placement handy to the kitchen door, though, as you will want to use them in cooking and baking. Most herbs can be planted in pots, and a large pot with several different types of herbs can be charming on a patio. Mix them according to size and watering needs. Chives, fennel, and borage can become invasive, however, so even if you plant them in pots, be sure to deadhead the flowers before they go to seed. Feverfew is considered to be an herb, but with its tiny, daisylike flowers, it will add interest to any area of your cottage garden. Feverfew does spread easily, and readily self-seeds, but unwanted plants can simply be removed and given away or composted.

And while we are thinking of putting herbs in our cottage garden, let's also address the possibility of including vegetables. If you don't have room for—or need—a large, formal vegetable plot, mix some vegetables in with your perennials. By choosing vegetable varieties carefully, you can complement the foliage of the perennials with the foliage of the vegetables. There are some small bush beans that would look lovely tucked in beside low-growing perennials such as lithodora. Or plant a cherry or grape tomato in with the sweet woodruff for a spot of color as the tomatoes ripen. Some of the new lettuces have attractive multicolored leaves and can give interest to an otherwise lackluster area of your sun garden. Remember to plant your vegetables so as to allow for easy cultivation and harvest. Corn and eggplant are impractical for most coastal gardens as the heat units just aren't there to ripen them. For this reason, tomatoes are also tricky and should be chosen with an eye for early ripening varieties. Potatoes can sometimes work well in a coastal cottage garden, but their foliage tends to die back and look unsightly when the rest of the garden is in its prime. The solution is to dig the potatoes when they reach this stage as it is also a sign of ripeness.

ROSES?

Most true English or American cottage gardens will have at least one rose. Many have been trained to climb an arbor, a trellis or the home itself. Can you do roses on the coast? Certainly, but with a few guidelines to make your job easier.

When you are choosing a rose, try to find one with a low petal count. These will fully open sooner. Choose a rose that is disease and insect resistant. "Resistant" doesn't mean immune. But it will at least help with the fungal diseases like black spot and mildew that are prevalent on the coast.

When planting your rose, it will need at least six hours of sunlight per day, more if possible. They like a well-drained, sandy-loam type of soil. Roses should be protected from the winds, especially the more delicate hybrid tea roses. Leave lots of space between each rose for air circulation, again to combat fungal diseases. Roses like about one gallon of water each week, and they don't like wet foliage, so water at the base. Mulch around the base to prevent the roots from becoming dry between watering, but don't let the mulch touch the stem of the plant. This encourages small animals to tunnel to the rose and feast on the tender bark.

If you live close to the ocean where your roses will be subject to salt-laden winds, try to wash the salt from the leaves periodically. Do this early on a sunny, dry day so that the leaves will dry off before sundown.

Clean dead or spotted leaves from around the base of the plants. This will also keep fungal diseases from spreading. You may also need to spray with a copper-based fungicide every two weeks or so. Remove any dead or diseased leaves from the plant at this time as well. Your plant may look a little sparse for a few days, but soon new leaves will sprout. Feed during the growth period (mid-spring to mid-August) with a systemic rose food that also includes a fungicide and insect repellant. A healthy plant will be better able to fight diseases and insects. Aphids will be your biggest threat, but are easily removed with a squirt of strong water or by gently rubbing them off the rose buds with your fingers.

Cut back in the late fall to about 24 inches, once the plants go dormant. If your roses are in a windy area, consider tying the canes together to keep them from whipping around in the wind and damaging the bush. In many milder climate areas along the coast, the roses will not go completely dormant. Still, hold off feeding until you can see active growth in the spring. This is also the time to move any roses you want to relocate. Prune again in mid-February for a bushier, healthier plant in the summer.

The best idea for roses, however, is to use *Rosa rugosa* and its hybrids. They are easy to grow and have adapted nicely to coastal conditions, not being bothered by the wind or the salt. They are virtually disease and pest resistant, but they can also get quite large and thorny. Pull out volunteers before they spread. Great for rose hips, too.

COTTAGE DUNE GARDENS

Although most of the cottage gardens seen on the coast are nestled into the mountains, these types of gardens are not exclusive to the higher elevations. Many of us still want the cottage garden in our sandy-soiled yards. This will be a little harder to create, but it can still be done using plants that have adapted to the harsh dune habitats.

A cottage dune garden can be an excellent way to use native plants in a creative way. Using natives can have a pleasing effect as long as they are not overplanned and overplanted. A natural-looking setting is the

Pond garden by the sea

Coastal Gardening in the Pacific Northwest

best design for a native garden. And its not as difficult as it seems, especially if you are lucky enough to have a property with standing native trees and shrubs.

Native plants such as salal, shore pines, California wax myrtle, and Pacific madrone can be lovely used as the bones of a cottage garden. All do well at the shore. Perennials like *Aquilegia* (columbine), penstemon, and fringecup (*Tellima grandiflora*) can be floral additions to the cottage garden if protected from the salt-laden winds. They have the added benefit of being long blooming and having interesting foliage as well. Generally, plants with narrow leaves do better in the saltier areas of the dunes.

If you have a shade garden, remember the native ferns make a lovely "grotto" effect. Sword ferns (*Polystichum munitum*) are evergreen. I just cut mine back in late February or early March before the new fronds start to emerge. It keeps the ferns from having the dead look when the older fronds turn brown. Lady ferns (*Athyrium filix-femina*) are deciduous and are best cut back in the late fall once they have browned as well. Our native deer fern (*Blechnum spicant*) are also pretty and easy to use in a shade garden. Maidenhair ferns (*Adiantum* spp.) have lovely foliage but are deciduous.

Myrica californica (Pacific wax myrtle)

There are many nonnative ferns that also do well at the coast. Japanese holly fern (*Cyrtomium falcatum*) likes either wet or dry soil, and may not be hardy for a mountainous area but will do well in a coastal Zone 8. The fronds are a dark, glossy green and have a holly look to them. The *Dryopteris* ferns are a great family and can be very diverse and unusual in their frond shape. My favorites are the male ferns, *D. affinis cristata*, a crested fern with gorgeous foliage that curls at the ends and is very upright in its growing habit. I must give you fair warning, however: once you begin exploring the wide world of ferns, you will become addicted and want one of everything.

Arbutus menziesii (Pacific madrone) flower

ADDITIONAL PLANTS FOR A COTTAGE DUNE GARDEN

Most of the plants we have discussed in the sections on dune gardens, Japanese-style, or Mediterranean gardens would do well in a cottage garden if planted in mass amounts. In addition, here are others.

Trees and Shrubs

Pinus contorta contorta (shore pine), *Myrica californica* (Pacific wax myrtle), *Fraxinus oregona* (Oregon ash), *Mahonia aquilfolium* (Oregon

grape), *Escallonia,* laurel, *Buxus* (boxwood), *Chamaecyparis lawsoniana*
(Port Orford cedar), *Picea abies* (Norway spruce), *Pinus sylvestris* (Scotch
pine), *Pinus thunbergii* (Japanese black pine), *Pseudotsuga menziesii*
(Douglas fir), *Salix discolor* (pussy willow), *Sambucus racemosa* (red elderberry), *Gaultheria shallon* (salal), rhododendron, and azalea.

*Dryopteris filix-
mas cristata
(crisped crested
male fern)*

Pieris japonica (**lily of the valley bush**): This very nice evergreen
plant has an upright growing habit and pretty hanging flowers that resemble lily of the valley. It likes the same conditions as rhododendrons:
acidic, well-drained soil, and cool summers. It does need shelter from
strong winds, though, and doesn't like salt-laden soil. Given proper
conditions it can get quite tall (9 to 10 feet) but adjusts well to pruning
after it blooms. Older plants can be thinned, if desired, by removing
whole branches.

Spirea: A group of deciduous shrubs that are wind resistant and
somewhat salt resistant. Some varieties bloom during the spring, others
in the summer. Many have colorful fall foliage, making this an interesting garden addition throughout most of the year.

Heaths (*Erica* spp.) and Heathers (*Calluna* spp.): Both of these
groups of plants make nice mounding shrubs good for a cottage garden
but also in Mediterranean- and Japanese-style gardens. They are easy to
grow on the coast and there is a wide variety of colors available. They

need acidic soil and will do best in full sun. By choosing a variety of bloom times, the heathers and heaths will provide color almost all year.

Salix alba vitellina 'Britzensis' (coral embers willow): If you have had trouble with the red-twigged dogwood suffering from coastal winds, try a coral embers willow. It, too, is deciduous and has reddish bark on the new stems, good fall color, and nice summer foliage. A member of the willow family, it will withstand wet soils and does well in the wind. For best branch color, cut it back hard in early spring as you would the red-twigged dogwood to force new, colorful growth.

Perennials

Giant reed grass, feather reed grass, sedges, corkscrew rush, northern sea oats, sand verbena, brunnera, aquilegia, yarrow, sedums, fringecup, penstemon, phormium, lupines, acanthus, aconitum, bergenia, sword ferns, lady ferns and many other ferns, clematis, trumpet vines, honeysuckles, wisterias, daylilies, pelargoniums.

Annuals and Tender Plants

Dahlias, *Veronica* (speedwell), *Centaurea cineraria* (dusty miller), *Lathyrus* (sweet peas), geraniums, *Tropaeolum majus* (nasturtium), and *Antirrhinum majus* (snapdragons).

Phormium (New Zealand flax)

ADDITIONAL PLANTS FOR A
COTTAGE-STYLE MOUNTAIN GARDEN

Trees and Shrubs

Dwarf fruit trees such as cherry, plum, or apple. Peaches can be grown on the coast but are a little fussier because their limbs tend to be fragile and break easily in the wind. Also blackberries, currants, raspberries, if given proper conditions.

Prunus x subhirtella (weeping cherry), *Acer palmatums* (Japanese maples), *Hamamelis mollis* (witch hazels), *Clerodendrum trichotomum*, hardy fuchsia, *Berberis*, heathers, *Ceanothus*, *Choisya* (Mexican orange), *Euonymous*, *Hebe*, *Hydrangea*, shrub or climbing roses, clematis, *Callicarpa* (beautyberry), Mahonias, *Sarcococca* (sweet box), *Spirea*, *Viburnum*, *Weigela*.

Perennials

Asters, lavenders, mallows (instead of hollyhocks, which have a tendency toward rust and mildew), sedum, *Nepeta*, *Acanthus*, *Stachys*, *Achillea*, *Aconitum*, *Coreopsis*, Shasta daisies, phlox, campanula, delphinium (or larkspur), nasturtium, *Alchemilla mollis*, anemones, aquilegia, astilbe, bergenia, chamomile, dahlias, dicentra, echinacea, euphorbia, geraniums, *Helleborus*, hostas, *Monarda* (bee balm), *Tradescantia virginiana* (spiderwort), *Penstemon*, ferns and grasses, *Helianthus* (annual sunflowers).

Roses

Rosa rugosa (native shrub roses), 'Simplicity' (pink), 'Honor' (white), 'Show Biz' and 'Climbing Blaze' (reds).

Vegetables and Herbs

Tomatoes (cherry and grape do best), bush beans, lettuces ("Freckles"), sorrel, lavender, sage, purple sage, parsley, thyme, rosemary, borage, fennel, mints, feverfew, onion, asparagus, artichokes, carrots, runner beans, peas, radishes.

PLANTS FOR A COTTAGE-STYLE RIPARIAN GARDEN

Almost any of the plants listed for a dune or mountain cottage garden can be used along streams and rivers. The key here will be to choose plants that fit the sunlight conditions and will grow if their roots are damp, like the native salals and rushes. The danger here with a lot of plantings along the streambeds is the possibility of winter floods. Do avoid planting noxious or invasive weeds that have been choking riparian areas such as the buddleia and the Japanese knotweed. Weeds that do well along riverbanks seem to become more of a problem than if they were in fields.

FIVE

VEGETABLES

AVING A VEGETABLE GARDEN on the Pacific Northwest coast can be an ordeal, but with a little work and planning, it can also be very rewarding. There is a special triumph in sitting down to a dinner made with produce you have nurtured from seedlings. Getting your family involved at the planning stage also makes it more likely they will help—and enjoy helping—throughout the process. There are some guidelines to follow that will give you a more successful vegetable garden.

To begin, the family should sit down with a note pad and jot down their ideas. Have each person answer every question and compare notes when everyone is done. By using your family's input, you will be guided toward a better end product, both in the garden and at harvest time.

First, decide how large a garden you need. Ask yourselves: "Why am I planting vegetables? It is for the experience and the excitement of growing something from seed?" (Hopefully it also will be because you will use the food for canning, freezing, or eating fresh.) "Will we be able to use all the produce or will we have to give some away? (You may consider planting an extra row of each crop to give to the local food banks. Helping others in this way can be especially rewarding to children in the family, and to adults as well.) How many people will we be feeding in our own family? What do we like to eat? Who will be helping? How much time and energy do we have to put into vegetables? Do we want to plant seeds or buy transplants at a nursery? How will we water the garden? How much time do we have to water the garden? How much time to weed and control pests? Will we want to fertilize? Who will do this task? What kind of a harvest can we expect?"

More practical questions arise: "What is the size of the site? Where will it be? Close to the house and/or close to the water source?" (Ideally, it should be close to both.) "Is there a slope to the site? Do we need to consider terracing or contour planting? How much sun does the site have? How much wind? Is it well drained?"

Once you all have asked and answered these questions, you can make some informed choices for your vegetable garden.

SITE SPECIFICS

The vegetables will prefer full sun if at all possible, and this means at least six hours a day. I find a vegetable garden close to the house is used more just because it is handy to weed, water, and harvest. Of course, this is not always practical, but do try to locate it so you will enjoy working in it and not have it be too far to walk or haul water. Along the south wall of your house or garage is good, too, to reflect heat back onto the plants. This is especially helpful if the walls are a light color. Orient your rows from north to south so the plants won't shade each other from the sun.

The next step after the location has been chosen is to prepare the soil. And those wonderful raised beds once again make life simpler. By constructing raised beds, we can more closely monitor and control soil amendments, water and nutrients. Raised beds have the added benefit of warming the soil earlier in the growing season and keeping it warmer longer into the autumn. They also can be built as platforms that are high enough to allow for standing or sitting to work on your garden. This is especially helpful for older gardeners who may have limited mobility. If raised beds are above ground level, drill holes in the bottom of the beds for drainage. Regular irrigation will be even more crucial, though, as these beds are basically raised containers and will dry out sooner than beds placed on the ground.

Your vegetables will prefer a soil pH of about 6.5, more neutral than most Pacific Northwest gardens, and by using raised beds, you can use compost and sulfur to sweeten the soil. Once again, you will need to test the soil for pH before you try to correct it. A simple test kit from the garden store will do, or you can take a soil sample to most county extension offices for testing. See directions in chapter 1 as to how to best collect your soil for testing.

You may also decide at this time that drip irrigation is a good fit for your garden. Do not use overhead sprays, as most vegetables tend to prefer being watered at their bases. Even if you choose to water by hand, try not to wet the foliage too much, aiming for the roots instead.

Plate 1.   *Buxus* (boxwood), *Euonymous fortunei* 'Emerald 'n Gold'
with *Rhododendron* ssp.

Plate 2.   *Solidago spathulata* (Coast goldenrod)

Plate 3. A Japanese-style garden

Plate 4. *Acer palmatum* 'Sangu Kaku' (Coral bark Japanese maple)

Plate 5. *Acer palmatum dissectum* 'Crimson Queen' (Japanese maple)

Plate 6. *Imperata cylindrica* 'Rubra' 'Red Baron' (Japanese blood grass)

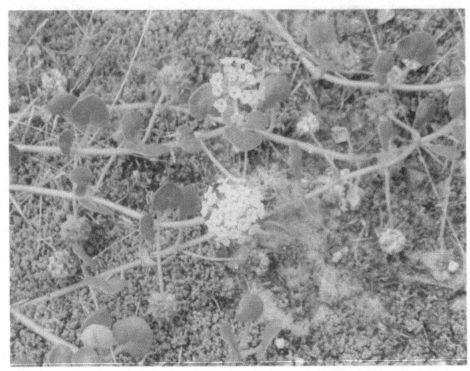

Plate 7. *Abronia latifolia* (sand verbena)

Plate 8. *Skimmia japonica* berries

Plate 9.   *Cyperus alternifolius* (Umbrella Grass)

Plate 10.   Fog moves over a Mediterranean garden

Plate 11.   Mediterranean garden with rudbeckia and lavender

Plate 12.   *Agastache*

Plate 13.   *Rhododendron* ssp.

Plate 14.   *Pinus contorta contorta* (Shore pine)

Plate 15.   Unknown coastal wild aster

Plate 16.   *Clematis*

Plate 17.   An American cottage garden

Plate 18.   A blue and pink color scheme is used in this cottage garden

Plate 19.   Blue accents create a whimsical sitting area

Plate 20.   A sundial adds a focal point

Plate 21.   *Holodiscus discolor* (ocean spray)

Plate 22.
Blue hydrangea ssp.

Plate 23.   *Tibouchina urvilleana* (princess flower shrub)

Plate 24.   *Erica* (unknown heather)

Plate 25. *Bergenia*

Plate 26. *Dryopteris erthrosora* (autumn fern)

Plate 27.   *Lavatera* (mallow)

Plate 28.   *Sedum* 'Autumn Joy'

Plate 29. *Anemone japonica* (Japanese anemone)

Plate 30. Dahlia 'Lavender Perfection'

Plate 31. *Cytisus scoparius* (Scotch broom) can grow to seven feet if left unattended

Plate 32.   Calla lilies

And a thorough watering twice a week will encourage deeper root growth and is preferable to a light watering daily.

Timing of when to start seeds or put out transplants can be complicated. To simplify things a bit, take a calendar for the coming year and use it to decide when to plant each vegetable that you want to try. Use the catalogs and any other reference information you have about each plant. Don't forget to take into account the microclimate of your garden. You may need to add a week—or even two—to the estimated time for planting. Or, if you are in a slightly warmer area, you may be able to put those plants out a few days earlier. Your local extension office can tell you the average dates of the last frost and you can then work from that date. By being just a little bit organized, you can avoid missing a planting opportunity.

Different vegetables will require different fertilizing. Using the seed catalogs, the backs of the seed packets themselves, or other references, make a list of when to fertilize each crop. Your calendar may come in handy for this task as well as a planting guide.

Decide if you will be planting seeds of each crop, buying plants to transplant into the garden, or a combination of both. Growing from seed will mean a longer commitment as most seeds will need to be started inside early in the spring, some as early as February. But it is also fun for the children to see a seed sprout. You will need a window with a lot of sunlight, or special grow lights. Many good books geared to all ages have been written on starting vegetables from seed. They will also list materials needed as well as potential problems and solutions. Propagating from seed takes patience, but it is also a less expensive alternative.

Purchasing plants from a greenhouse will give you a good head start on those longer season vegetables like tomatoes and peppers. You will need to harden off your plants whether they are coming directly from a grower or your own greenhouse or window. "Hardening off" simply involves putting the plants outside during the warm days and bringing them into shelter at night. Do this for 10 to 14 days before moving them into the vegetable beds. It is generally safe to put them into the garden beds when the soil temperature reaches about 55 degrees. This temperature will be reached sooner in the season if you are using our old friend, raised beds.

Even if you purchase good-sized plants, still try to find varieties that have a short time to maturity. Usually 50 to 70 days is preferred for coastal gardens. The best place for information about the length of time until harvest is in one of the regional seed catalogs. They are excellent reference guides. Of course, you can also purchase seed from them, especially if you have good growing conditions to start seeds indoors or in a greenhouse. I recommend using one of the Pacific Northwest seed producers, as they are more familiar with what will do well here than seed companies elsewhere.

MAINTENANCE

Vegetables are not maintenance-free plants. They need to be watered on a regular basis and fertilized at specific times during their growing season. The soil needs to be improved each year. Each separate vegetable has its own list of needs. But they are well worth the effort when you pick that first ripe grape tomato, harvest the first beans of the season, or make a salad using produce from your own garden.

Near the top of the maintenance list is weeding. Though some gardeners enjoy the process of weeding, it can often be a chore. If your garden is not large you may be able to run a hoe through the rows daily to take care of any weeds that have sprouted since the day before. More realistically, you will only have time to weed the entire garden once a week, and that's if you are lucky enough to find the time to do that much. There are few things worse than approaching a neglected vegetable patch that has weeds choking the beans or the peas. Its hard to know where to begin and harder yet to know how long to plan for weeding. As a result we dread the task and we put it off for another day or two, making matters worse. But if you take 15 minutes each morning before you go to work, or 15 minutes each evening before dark and weed a different row each day, you will be ahead of the game. You will no longer feel guilty about deserting your garden, and in fact daily weeding may give you a release from the tensions of your day.

COMPANION, CONTOUR, AND SUCCESSION PLANTING

Companion planting can best be described as placing certain plants together in the garden to increase the yields of each. Some plants naturally do well together. Others naturally will harm each other if grown too close. By carefully planning out your vegetable plot on paper, you can avoid putting "enemies" together and make "friendly" plants neighbors.

Other plants—such as some herbs and flowers—can be beneficial when planted in the vegetable garden, too. Borage deters undesirable worms and improves growth and flavor of many vegetables. It also strengthens strawberries' resistance to insects and diseases. When planted as a border around strawberries, thyme can deter cabbage worms. Marigolds help to discourage beetles and nematodes. Nasturtiums deter aphids, beetles, and bugs, including squash bugs, and will improve the growth of radishes. Nasturtium flowers are edible and their bright colors make a lovely and delicious addition to any salad. Oregano provides a general pest protection to many vegetables. Basil not only repels flies but can improve flavor and growth to tomatoes. Chamomile improves the flavor and growth of the onion family. Dill can improve growth in the cabbage family but when mature, acts as a growth retardant to tomatoes. Catnip, sage, mint, and rosemary can discourage the cabbage moths that attack that family. Rosemary and sage can also deter carrot flies. When arranging your companion plants, remember to take into account how tall they will be at maturity. For example, don't plant the pole beans so they will shade the carrots or radishes from the sun.

There is a list at the end of this chapter for examples of good and bad plant combinations.

Contour planting can be effective if you have a curving hillside with a slope for your garden area. This technique helps to avoid soil erosion and basically consists of planting in narrow, level terraces that follow the curve of the hillside. You can use landscape timbers, rocks, or bricks to hold the soil in the terraces. Since this involves working along a hillside, though, you must firmly secure each level as well as provide for drainage so the terraces won't collapse in the first winter rain.

Succession planting can be described as planting something new in the space left by plants that have reached maturity and have stopped producing. For example, early crops such as beets, lettuce, and early cabbages can be harvested and leave space in the garden for beans or tomatoes. Radishes can make way for peppers or tomatoes. When the beans are finished, plant an area with fall cabbages or carrots. Spring vegetables make room for summer vegetables, which in turn make room for fall or winter crops. Remember, though, that the soil will be depleted by each succession of crops and so must be reconditioned before replanting.

CROP ROTATION

A very important aspect of having a healthy vegetable garden from year to year is making certain to rotate your crops—and crop families—each season. This may sound like a lot of additional planning for the vegetable garden, but it will prove worth your while if you can resist planting the same vegetables in the same spot for at least three years. Doing so will help combat not only insect infestations, but diseases.

Insects have food preferences and will even lay their eggs or larvae near where they know their youngsters will have access to a good meal once they hatch. By moving the families of plants each season, we will confuse the insects and buy the vegetables a little more time to develop before the insects or their larvae can find them again.

Identification of the invading insect is also important so we can interrupt the food cycle before crops are damaged to the point of being unable to survive. Each type of insect has its most damaging developmental stage. Some are more voracious as larvae, others as adults. Look for more specifics on this topic in chapter 6, "Potential Problems."

Diseases are another reason to rotate crops. There are three factors that have to be present for a disease to infect a plant. The first factor is that the disease pathogen needs to be present. The second factor is the presence of a host plant. The third factor is the proper environment for the disease pathogen to grow. For example, in the Pacific Northwest, fungal diseases need to have their spores and specific host plants present. They also require a cool, damp environment—including rainfall—to grow and spread. By moving the host plant, we interrupt the cycle and the disease has no way to get the nutrients it needs to spread and reproduce its fungal spores.

Usually a three-year rotation is sufficient for most crops. When you are rotating, be certain not to plant the same families in the same areas, as well. Cabbages and Brussels sprouts, for instance, should not replace each other, nor should cauliflowers and kales, nor tomatoes, potatoes, and peppers be planted in the same area for the three-year period.

PLANT CHOICES

As we have discussed many times so far, the choice of plants is crucial to any successful garden; this is also true of vegetables and fruits.

Perhaps the easiest way to start discussing plant choices is to talk about vegetables to avoid. The Pacific Northwest coastal areas have generally cooler summers, so plants that need a lot of heat to set fruit are more difficult to grow here than the same plants would be to grow even 30 miles inland. Forget about corn, melons, sweet potatoes, and eggplant. Concentrate on the ones that can be grown and you won't be disappointed in your crops.

Lettuces, peas, and other cool-weather crops are excellent choices for a Pacific Northwest vegetable garden. And in most years, you can have more than one planting, sowing an additional crop in early September. By the time the lettuce has sprouted, the cool weather will have returned and the plants will thrive. In the United States and Canada, newly popular types of crops for cool weather are Asian vegetables such as pak choi (or bok choy), Tah Tsai, and Chinese cabbages. These have the added benefit of being able to try fun new recipes to use these interesting vegetables. Read the seed packets for harvest information as some are best when left to bolt, while others are picked earlier than usual to avoid getting tough.

Summer and winter squash are also good growers on the coast. Again choose with time-to-harvest dates in mind. They also need the sunniest location possible and starting the seeds early indoors is again a benefit.

One of the most fun and exotic vegetables to grow is the artichoke. These dramatic plants do take up a good bit of space in the garden, however, so be sure you like to eat them before you plant them. A good artichoke plant will produce three or more chokes each year and can be left in the ground over the winter.

A list of specific vegetable varieties for the Pacific Northwest coast appears at the end of this chapter.

TOMATOES

The question I hear most often is, "Can I grow a nice tomato here?" My answer is often a question in return: "What do you mean by a nice tomato?" If your idea of a good tomato is a huge 'Big Boy' or 'Beefsteak', probably not. But if you like the sweet taste of a smaller cherry or grape tomato, have at least six hours of full sun, and can protect them from the wind . . . absolutely "yes!"

Most people moving to the Pacific Northwest coast or beginning gardeners here want to grow tomatoes. Tomatoes are problematic but not impossible. Again, selecting the best varieties and choosing tomatoes that have a short time to maturity will produce the best results. Most seed packages will contain the "days to harvest" information, but this won't always be available when you buy a plant at a nursery, so know which varieties to look for when you go shopping.

Oregon State University has developed several good varieties that will set fruit in cooler climates. 'Siletz' has a maturity date of 70 to 75 days as does 'Early Cascade'. OSU's 'Legend' tomato harvests in 68 days and is a nice-tasting, smaller tomato. 'Oregon Spring' takes about 75 to 80 days, but 'Northern Delight' and 'Santiam' only take about 65 to 70 days.

Forget about trying to grow the huge varieties like 'Brandywine' and 'Beefsteak' because they simply take too long to ripen. My in-laws have the theory that fruits and vegetables only have so much flavor to go around, so the smaller the fruit, the fuller the taste. This, of course, is not always true, but it seems to work for tomatoes. Smaller fruiting varieties such as cherry, plum, and grape tomatoes have concentrated tomato flavor and are excellent choices. They will generally outperform the larger-fruited varieties in our cooler climates. Try 'Golden Nugget' or 'Honeybunch' in a large planter on the patio in full sun and you'll be picking them to eat right off the vine.

You may find that early producing tomatoes use a great amount of calcium. Here is another instance where a soil test comes in handy. If your garden starts out low in calcium, amend it by adding bone meal or calcium nitrate, or by liming the garden in the autumn before spring planting. Liming has the added benefit of sweetening acidic soil to a more desirable pH for tomatoes, too.

If you are buying tomato transplants rather than starting them from seed, be certain to choose healthy, bushy plants with dark green leaves and no signs of disease or insect damage. Tall plants can be planted deeper into the ground, and their stems will grow roots under the ground. But spindly or yellow-green-leaved plants should be passed by. When the weather has warmed sufficiently, harden your new plants off before planting them in the ground. As mentioned before, this is done by leaving them in the sun for an increasing amount of time each day, bringing them into shelter at night. Don't be tempted to start this process too early. You will want the daytime temperatures to be constantly in the upper 60s or low 70s and the soil temperature to be 50 to 55 degrees. The purchase of a soil thermometer is a good investment, but only if you remember to use it.

Once the tomatoes are placed in the ground, they will start to develop new branches. Some of these lower branches will not produce fruit and are called "suckers." These should be removed so the energy of the plant can be better spent producing fruit. Continue to remove suckers throughout the season as they appear. If you are planting in a container, choose "determinate" varieties. These are usually shorter, bushier types of tomatoes and will set fruit once they have reached their genetically predetermined size. They tend to have more of a horizontal growth pattern. "Indeterminate" plants will grow more vertically and continue to set fruit until the first frost. These are best planted into the ground with strong supports such as cages or stakes. Look for this information on seed packets or in catalogs because the nursery-grown plants will generally not have this information either.

Maximize the warmth at the growing site for the best crop of tomatoes. This can be done by growing in greenhouses, raised beds, straw beds, row covers, or cloches. Choose the sunniest possible site. In a warmer microclimate, row covers will have to be removed before the heat of the day. This will prevent withering from too much heat. But if row covers need to be left on in a cooler climate, shake the plants during midday to facilitate pollination. This process is normally done by the winds, but of course under row covers, there is no wind.

Many gardeners are having success with using red plastic to mulch their tomatoes. Using these mulches at the base of the tomato plants will hold in the heat but will also limit the amount of water the plants receive, so monitor water needs if you decide to try the plastic mulches. When watering, keep the foliage dry but the soil moist. Using drip irrigation at the base will help prevent fungal diseases that so plague us on the Pacific Coast. If watering by hand, wet the ground evenly and regularly to produce the best crop. Once the fruit has started to set, hold off on watering. If possible, cover the plants during heavy rains.

Tomatoes are notoriously susceptible to a host of fungal diseases such as early blight, late blight, and botrytis. To avoid some of these problems, plant the tomatoes far enough apart—from each other as well as other vegetables—to allow good circulation. Check the plants daily or every few days, and at the first sign of a problem remove and destroy the infected plants. Once infected a plant cannot be cured and so should be removed. Preventative fungicides are available, and ones labeled for use on tomatoes can be applied every 7 to 14 days, stopping at least a week or more before harvest. Fixed copper sprays can prevent late blight and neem oil sprays prevent gray mold and early blight. Both are acceptable for use in organic gardens and are available in garden centers.

Staying on a strict regiment of crop rotation will also help to decrease disease and insect problems. For tomatoes, peppers, and potatoes this means not planting any of them in the same area for at least three years.

With a bit of diligence and some trial and error, tomatoes can be worthwhile additions to your vegetable beds. And there is nothing like the taste of that first tomato fresh from the vine, warm from the sun, in August.

PLANT SUGGESTIONS

Here I have listed several varieties of vegetables that have proven to do well in coastal conditions. You may have to do some trials for yourself to see which work best in your microclimate but this is at least a starting point.

ARTICHOKES: Provide shelter from wind. Mulch to overwinter.
  Green Globe'—Early summer flowering with harvest of three to four heads throughout the summer.

'Imperial Star'—Suited for mountain gardens if grown as annual. Will be a perennial in Zone 7 or higher.

BEANS (POLE):

'Blue Lake Pole'—Excellent flavor, good production, good for canning or fresh.

'Kentucky Wonder'—Great flavor and production. Heirloom; 70 days to harvest.

French/Filet 'Nickel'—Beautiful and delicious as well. Very thin and long. Harvest when less than a quarter inch diameter for best flavor and tenderness.

BEANS (BUSH): Look for ones resistant to anthracnose, mosaic viruses, and rust.

'Totem'—Good canning bush bean.

BEETS: May need extra boron. Go by the results of your soil test.

'Detroit Dark Red'—Recommended by coastal gardeners.

'Early Wonder'—Popular beet; vigorous growth in cold soils. Also pickles well.

BROCCOLI: Beach gardeners may not be able to mature. For best results use transplants and set them out in April or May.

'Green Comet'—Good producer and lots of side shoots once the leader was removed. Looser buds than some.

'Umpqua'—Plant as early as March to avoid bolting. Long harvest. 60 days.

'Packman'—Early maturation of 55 days. Effective even when grown organically, but may need to be amended with bone meal for best organic results. Tall plant; tight, uniform crowns.

BRUSSELS SPROUTS: Plant around June 1 for a winter crop.

'Bubbles'—Good taste, extended harvest because of good field-holding ability. Tolerates warm weather and has some drought resistance. About 88–92 days to harvest.

CABBAGE: Watch for pests such as slugs, flea beetles, and cabbage moth larvae. Use floating row covers to protect from insect pests.

'Parel'—Mild, sweet flavor. Field-holds up to three weeks. Short season of 50 days.

CARROTS: Some usual varieties are small in coastal gardens. Overwintering types are best. To prevent wireworm and rust fly, use floating row covers.

'Nantes' or 'Nantaise'—Medium long, uniform, sweet taste. Sixty-eight days to harvest.

'Thumbelina'—60 days to harvest. Bite-sized, nugget-shaped baby carrot. Excellent color and flavor.

CAULIFLOWER: Can be produced April through November on most of coast. Start seeds mid-March to mid-June.

'**Snow Crown**'—Mild, sweet. Rapid, easy growth. Field-hold up to 10 days. Time to harvest: 50 to 60 days.

'**Early Dawn SG**'—Good for maritime northwest gardens. Short-season of 53 days. Field-held for 7 to 10 days.

CHARD (AKA SWISS CHARD): Good early planting crop. May even get second season if planted in late August.

'**Bright Lights**'—not likely to bolt until later in the season. Sixty days to harvest. Each stem colored differently—red, orange, yellow, white—for lovely growth. Mild flavors.

'**Bright Yellow**'—Mild and sweet. Sixty days to harvest.

CUCUMBER (PICKLING): Prefers full sun and well-drained soil.

'**County Fair**'—Disease resistant, wonderful for pickling at six to eight-inch size. Carries bitter-free, burp-less gene.

CUCUMBER (SLICING):

'**Lemon**'—most reliable producer in coastal gardens. Unique taste and round shape. Mild flesh, sweet without a bitter taste. Seventy days to harvest.

'**Poinsett 97**'—Disease tolerant, good for organic gardeners.

GARLIC: Almost all good on coast if well-drained soil. Needs a pH of about 6.5. Plant in early October for harvest the following summer. Harvest when only three or four green leaves are left on the stem for best results and storage.

'**Oregon Blue**'—Heirloom, good for coastal gardens, softneck. Mid-season producer. 8 to 10 cloves per bulb. Good storage.

KALE: Most of kale family does well on coast. It can tolerate frost after it has become established. Some are highly ornamental but others can also be used in salads and stir-fried dishes.

LETTUCES: Most leaf lettuce will do well in our cooler temperatures. Don't bother with heads unless you have a very warm spot and can plant early. Bait for slugs, though, which love the tender lettuce leaves.

'**Buttercrunch**'—Sweet tasting leaves; does okay in more acidic soil. Holds into autumn; long to bolt. Forty-eight days to harvest.

'**Red Sail**'—Colorful lettuce with loads of vitamins. Also does well in warmer weather. Fifty-three days to harvest. Will stay longer in gardens without bolting or becoming bitter.

'**Salad Bowl**'—Good in cooler weather, early sowing in garden. Rapid growth but resists bolting. Fifty days to harvest.

'**Gourmet Salad Blend**'—From Territorial Seeds. Blend of favorites: 'Slobolt', 'Valmaine', 'Buttercrunch', 'Red Sail', and 'Salad Bowl'. Makes a very pretty mixed lettuce plot that is lovely as a salad.

'Valmaine' (Romaine)—Heat tolerant, can be grown from spring into fall if done in successive plantings. Good for traditional Caesar salads.

ONIONS: Use bulblets when green for more tender results. Best results reported when wintering over. Chives are also a success on the coast but may thrive too much and run wild. Try to deadhead them before they go to seed to eliminate this problem.

'Walla Walla Sweet'—125 days if sown in the spring. Can also be sown in fall for larger bulbs. Sweet flavor, but do not store well.

'Sweet Winter'—Good for overwintering.

PAK CHOI (BOK CHOY): Same pests as regular cabbage.

'Ching Chiang'—Early, dwarf pak choi. Bred for tolerance of heat, rain, cold, damp, so good for coastal gardens.

'Joi Choi'—Large and fast-growing variety. Juicy, mild flavor. Sow in spring or fall. Slow to bolt. Forty-five days to harvest.

PARSNIPS: Winter food source. Sweet, long, white root crop. Grown similar to carrots.

'Hollow Crown'—Prefers a loamy soil with some manure as fertilizer.

PEAS: Chill the seeds for three days or soak them for one day before planting to enhance sprouting. Good for cool, coastal gardens.

'Corvallis'—Virus resistant.

'Maestro'—Good shelling pea, virus resistant, multiple crops.

'Novella II'—Needs no support. Heavy pod set, easy to harvest. Virus resistant.

'Oregon Sugar Pod II'—Edible pod pea. Prolific and easy to harvest. Virus resistant. Early planting possible in February. Harvest in 105 days. Prolific.

PEPPERS (BELL): Plant as early as possible; using transplants gives best results.

'Jingle Bells'—Small red bell pepper, good flavor and high producer.

'Big Bertha Bell'—Green turns to red, extra large.

'Golden Bell'—Vigorous bushy growth, sweet peppers. Juicy, thick walled. Good for any use. Harvest in 62 days.

'California Wonder 300'—65 days to harvest. Very sweet, four to five peppers per plant. Green turns to red on bush. Good stuffing pepper. Good even in cooler growing conditions.

PEPPERS (HOT): For the most heat, keep on the dry side once they start to ripen. All peppers like full sun and should be protected from the wind.

'Container Thailand Hot'—Ornamental as well as very hot. Covered with fleshy pods that are well used when a hot pepper is needed.

'Jalapeno Goliath'—Hotter than most but good flavor and texture as well as disease resistant.

'Poblano'—Excellent in Mexican cooking. Called "poblano" when fresh but "ancho" when dried.

'Serrano Chili'—Slender, dark green, but very hot. Very prolific but also lasts in fresh storage.

POTATOES (RED): No manure or lime needed. Likes sandier soil. Dig before fall rains. Planting in straw only draws the slugs easier. Planting the eyes of grocery store potatoes is a less expensive alternative to purchasing seed potatoes. If composted, the potato scraps may also sprout, creating "volunteer" plants.

Red Pontiac'—Lots of eyes but good flavor and production.

POTATOES (WHITE):

'Norgold Russet'—A longtime favorite white potato.

POTATOES (YELLOW):

'Yukon Gold'—Good yellow potato; Prolific. About 70 to 90 days to harvest. Has outstanding flavor and dry texture.

'Yellow Firm'—Delicious flavor and does well at the coast. Keeps well.

PUMPKINS: Give lots of room and beware of squash bugs and powdery mildew. Water along feeder roots of the vine.

'Jack-o-Lantern'—Good crop, sweet flavor.

'Magic Lantern'—Nice sized pumpkin, good for carving. Early crop, compact vines, tolerant to powdery mildew.

'Small Sugar'—Smaller fruits, heirloom, sweet flavor, good for baking.

RADISHES: All types, but protect from root maggots with floating row covers.

RHUBARB: Likes well-drained, deep, rich soil, if possible. Bait for slugs. Cut off any blossom stalks for better crop. These stalks are also a sign the plant should be divided.

'Crimson Red'—Perfect rhubarb flavor, sweet and tart. Winter hardy.

'Victoria'—Greenish-red stalks; early maturation; good for pies and cobblers.

SPINACH: Good cool weather crop for the coast.

'Bloomsdale Savoy'—Reliant producer, sweet, succulent leaves. Can be planted in fall for overwintering and to bloom in spring. But best sown in very early spring for late spring harvest; 50 days to harvest.

'Melody'—Smooth leaved variety.

'Tyee'—Large, vigorous growing leaf with good flavor, but bolts in very hot weather. Tolerant of most diseases.

SQUASH: May need reliable water to set fruit if not enough rain. Generally do well on coast, but male and female blossoms may not mature at same time, reducing pollination opportunities.

'Acorn'—May not mature in cool summers.

'Bush Table Queen'—Good harvest with a sweet flavor.

'Yellow Crookneck'—Does extremely well on the coast or inland gardens. About 65 days to maturity. Old-fashioned favorite. Cook when small for best flavor and tenderness. If let go too long, use as gourds.

'Zucchini'—Does well on the coast, even at the beach—but no surprise there!

'Seneca'—Good harvest and nice flavor.

'Black Beauty'—Pretty, dark skin. Harvest when young for tender results. Matures in 60 days. Best when six to eight inches long.

TOMATOES: Start plants early and set out in protected but sunniest possible area. Stop fertilizing in mid-July and stop watering in late August to better ripen the fruit. See the special section on tomatoes in this chapter.

'Early Cascade'—Indeterminate. Clusters of fruit, good tasting and good producer. About 70 to 75 days to maturity.

'Early Girl'—Indeterminate. Good early tomato for salads and slicing. About 75 to 80 days to harvest.

'Legend'—Determinate. Resistant of late blight. Earliest slicing tomato. Very sweet, uniform shape. Sixty-eight days to harvest.

'Northern Delight'—Bred for the far north at 65 days to harvest. Mellow, sweet flavor.

'Oregon Spring'—Determinate. Extra-early slicing tomato. May even be planted outside in mid-April in warmer areas and will continue to produce if protected from frost. May have thicker skins in cooler areas. About 75 to 80 days to harvest.

'Roma'—Determinate. Famous sauce or juice tomato. Elongated shape and meaty. Matures in 70 days.

'Santiam'—Smaller sister to Oregon Spring, but matures a week earlier at 65 to 75 days. Round, red, delicious tomato taste. Determinate.

'Siletz'—Determinate. Vigorous growth, nearly seedless, very flavorful. Reliable slicing tomato. Matures in 70 to 75 days.

'Heirloom Sunset's Red Horizon'—Heirloom. Large fruit, may fruit into November in protected coastal gardens. Resists blossom end rot and cracking. Delicious fruit.

TOMATOES (CHERRY, GRAPE, OR SMALLER):

'Gold Nugget'—Determinate. Vigorous and one of first small tomatoes to ripen. Very rich, sweet flavor, produces until frost. Sixty days to harvest.

'Honeybunch' (grape)—"Pole" Determinate, so it will produce throughout the season and will grow as tall as it is supported. Bite sized but big tomato taste. Clusters of 10 or more fruits.

'Sweet Million'—Indeterminate. Grape-like clusters on three-foot-tall plants. Disease resistant. Matures in 65 to 75 days.

'Sweetie'—Indeterminate. Early and much sweeter than Sweet 100. Cherry tomato with big tomato flavor. If protected in a green-house, 'Sweetie' can produce for years.

'Tumbler'—Determinate. Bushy plant developed for hanging baskets. High productivity. Early ripening.

COMPANION PLANTS

Here are a few possible pairings for your vegetables. I have also included ones to keep apart.

Bush beans: DO: Beets, potatoes, carrots, cucumbers, and cabbage. DON'T: members of the onion family such as leeks, onions, chives, or garlic.

Pole Beans: DO: Radishes, potatoes and marigolds. DON'T: Beets or onion family members.

Cabbage Family: DO: Beets, chard, cucumbers, lettuces, onion, potatoes, spinach, dill, nasturtium, thyme. DON'T: Tomatoes, which can stunt the growth of kohlrabi.

Carrots: DO: Beans, lettuce, onions, peas, radishes, tomatoes, chives. DON'T: Dill.

Chard: DO: Beans, cabbage family, and onions.

Cucumbers: DO: Beans, cabbage family, peas, radishes, tomatoes, marigolds, nasturtium, oregano. DON'T: Sage.

Garlic: DO: Cane fruits, tomatoes, roses, cabbages. DON'T: Peas and beans.

Lettuces: DO: Beets, cabbage family, carrots, onion, radishes, strawberries.

Onions: DO: Beets, cabbage family, carrots, chard, lettuce, peppers, strawberries, tomatoes. DON'T: Peas and beans.

Peppers: DO: Carrots, onions, tomatoes.

Potatoes: DO: Beans, cabbage family, peas, marigolds. DON'T: Tomatoes, which are susceptible to the same blight as potatoes.

Pumpkins: DO: Squash, Marigolds, nasturtiums, oregano.

Radishes: DO: Beans, carrots, cucumbers, lettuce, peas, nasturtium, chervil. DON'T: Hyssop.

Squash: DO: Pumpkin, borage, marigolds, nasturtiums, oregano.

Strawberries: DO: Beans, lettuce, onions, spinach, thyme, borage. DON'T: Cabbage.

Tomatoes: DO: Carrots, cucumbers, onion, parsley, peppers, basil, monarda, chives, mint, borage, marigolds. DON'T: Kohlrabi, potatoes.

SIX

POTENTIAL PROBLEMS

WHEN I STARTED WRITING THIS BOOK, I didn't think my second-longest chapter would be about problems. But as I began to address diseases, weeds, insects, and creatures, I realized that problems—and knowing how to deal with them—are a very important part of gardening on the coast or anywhere. So don't be discouraged by the length of this chapter. Use it instead as a guide to solving those problems.

As we know, living on the Pacific Northwest coast has many gardening advantages: the mild climate, the abundance of winter rain, and the resulting ability to grow a wide variety of plant matter. But it also brings its own set of problems that are unique to the geographical area. Weeds, insects, deer, elk, and moles all enjoy the same mild climate humans do. We will discuss a few in this chapter, and give some possible solutions to each.

WEEDS

"One man's flower is another man's weed." A familiar saying to gardeners and one that holds a lot of truth. A rose planted in the wrong spot could be considered a weed, and indeed the native *Rosa rugosa* is a perfect example. This rose makes a lovely shrub hedge, but it also sends out runners that will creep into the driveway and the other beds if left to do so. Many weeds have started as garden staples, such as English ivy, butterfly bush, and purple loosestrife, but have escaped the garden to become bullies and taken over the wild from native species. As responsible gardeners, if we already have such plants as the very invasive loosestrife, English ivy, or buddleia in our gardens, we must either remove them or make certain that we keep them under control and do not let them go to seed or in other ways get out of hand. If we do not have them, we should not purchase them. In fact, many states have quarantined some noxious weeds and it is illegal to sell or purchase these intruders.

Annoying versus Noxious

There are different ways of describing weeds, which indicates how much of a problem they can be. There are weeds that are simply annoying, like little bittercress or herb-robert. As bothersome as they are, they are easily pulled out and disposed of. Some weeds, like dandelions or red sorrel, are more troublesome, requiring a little more work and persistence to stay ahead of their spread. Other plants are aggressive and difficult to remove. Some varieties of bamboo or an escaped *Rosa rugosa* could be put into this category. Still others can be considered invasive because of their ability to strangle or take over from other plants. I would include the bindweeds and yellow flag iris in this division. And the most egregious weeds are considered to be noxious. Noxious weeds are a threat to the natural environment, and these include purple loosestrife. In fact, loosestrife has become such a problem in riparian areas that the United States federal government has placed it on a nationwide quarantine. Many of the Canadian provinces are in the process of doing so as well.

The majority of states and provinces have their own lists of noxious weeds. The list varies from state to state and province to province for obvious reasons: each area has its own climatic conditions that will keep some weeds under control but allow others to expand their territories. The states' lists are generally based on what plants have been imported from other regions of the country, or indeed the world, and have escaped cultivation to become a threat to native plants or commercial agricultural enterprises.

Each of our coastal states has ranked its weeds into at least two lists. Washington state has three classes, A, B, and C. California ranks their weeds as high-, medium-, and low-impact. British Columbia categorizes its weeds as having an effect on the entire province or only in designated regional districts. Oregon has a two-list system (class A and class B) with an added potential problem list that targets weeds with the capability of becoming noxious and so are targeted for immediate control.

One would think that the similar climates in British Columbia, Oregon, Washington, and Northern California would mean that the invasive plants lists would be identical. This is not the case. Plants such as Scotch broom, yellow star thistle and knapweeds are on everyone's lists.

But surprisingly, English ivy hasn't made the Canadian list and European beach grass isn't on the Oregon list. The best idea, then, is to contact your local extension office, your state's agriculture department, or its department of environmental resources for an updated list for your area. You can then go the extra step to help eradicate the problem weeds as well as not planting them in your garden.

A very wise nurserywoman once told me that it was the job of every plant to try to take over the world. While it may not be true of that fragile plant you have been nursing for three years to get it to bloom, it certainly is true of the weed population.

Weeds—like desirable garden plants—are generally annual or perennial. Annual weeds complete their reproductive cycle in one season. The seeds they produce will lay on the ground until conditions are right again to set roots and bloom and go back to seed. Perennial weeds are basically year-round problems and continue their cycles from year to year. Some weeds, like little bittercress, are considered to be annuals but have such a short span between seed productions that they will complete several cycles in a calendar year.

For many perennial weeds such as bindweed, English ivy, Himalayan blackberry, and the thistles, the roots are more problematic than the tops of the plants when it comes to removal. Root segments left in the ground will resprout in a few days and continue to be a problem. Many perennial plants become more aggressive at this stage and throw out even more plants from the segmented roots. To combat these types of long-rooted plants, we must be persistent. Repeatedly cutting or pulling of the stems and roots will eventually weaken the plant. Weeding after a rain is certainly easier than when the soil is dry and hard. But in the case of perennial, long-rooted weeds, the moist soil may help them resprout from the segmented roots that are left behind. Taking the extra time now to pull all the roots will save you weeding time in the long run.

Attacking the seeds of annual, biennial, or perennial weeds is a necessary step in control of most weeds. It is especially important not to let biennial (Queen Anne's lace, tansy ragwort, or ragweed) weeds even get to the flowering stage. Since these plants will not be around the following year, they tend to produce high volumes of seeds, making them harder to control. This is also true of annual weeds. Because they use a large amount of energy to grow, bloom, and produce seeds before they die, pulling annual plants at their flowering stage is the most effective weeding time, as it makes it difficult for them to regroup and reflower.

In addition, ungerminated weed seeds should not be composted but removed to the trash. Some types of weed seeds can be viable for 20 years or more. And weeds produce seeds at varying times of the year;

some can flower multiple times on a single stem. Weeds generally use more water, nutrients, and sun than most garden-desirable plants. Using mulch will deter most of those weed seeds from sprouting. The best to use are the organic types such as shredded, disease-free leaves, clean straw, or dried grass cuttings.

We will discuss a few weeds that are either current problems or have the potential to become a problem along the Pacific Coast.

English Ivy

The first villain most of us think of is English ivy (*Hedera helix*). Imported from Europe by well-meaning landscape designers, this plant was a staple in a lot of West Coast gardens. And in all fairness, in a colder climate, English ivy is a much better behaved plant. But on the coast, with the mild winters and lots of sun in the summer and rain in the winter, the ivy runs wild. You can often see it choking the trees in big city parks and suburbs. It has also escaped to roadside tree plantings and is gradually working its way into the forests. That's where it gets nasty. It grows equally well in sun or shade, which has become part of its problem. It's happy everywhere.

English ivy is not a parasite of the tree on which it climbs. It does not rob the trees and shrubs of their nutrients by attaching to the trunk. But it instead will grow so many leaves that it will eventually shade the tree's leaves from the sunlight. If the tree is thus unable to photosynthesize, it will not survive. In its mature stage, this weed takes on a different form. The immature heart-shaped leaves become elongated as the plant ages and will form white berries that the birds love and will deposit miles from the original plant. The simplest way to prevent the ivy from maturing is to regularly cut it back severely. Don't worry. Unless you remove all its roots as well, it will come back, thicker than ever.

If you do want to remove ivy from a tree, the "No Ivy League" of Portland suggests cutting the ivy stems from the tree at about ankle and shoulder height. Roll the cut ivy back from the tree base. If you can, dig gently around the tree to get out as many ivy roots as you can. Fortunately, they are generally shallow rooted, so this isn't difficult to do. If you can, gently pull the cut ivy from the branches you can easily reach as well. The ivy stems that are left high in the tree will eventually die and blow off in the wind. The ivy's leaves will have fallen, allowing the tree to once again photosynthesize. It may take a few sessions to remove the ivy, but its worth the effort in the end. You will almost be able to hear the tree give a sigh of relief as if it can breathe again. Chemicals are most often not effective, as you are dealing with surrounding plants that will also be killed by use of a herbicide.

Hedera helix
(English ivy) at
mature stage

Brooms

Another obvious weed along the coast is Scotch broom (*Cytisus sco-parius*). This plant originally was brought to Vancouver Island in 1850 by Captain Walter C. Grant, at the time a recent Scottish immigrant, who brought the first broom seeds from the British consul in Hawaii. From the original seeds, only three germinated and the descendants of those three have populated most of the southern part of Vancouver Island. In this relatively short amount of time that Scotch broom has been in North America, it has succeeded in encroaching along the roadsides. Some specimens have grown to heights of 10 to 15 feet. The brooms like full sun, so they are less likely than English ivy to creep into the forests. But because of its preference for full sun and the fact that it tolerates sandy soil, it is becoming a problem on the ocean dunes. It creates a dense thicket that crowds out native wildlife as well as native plants. In full bloom, Scotch broom's pretty, deep-yellow flowers are unmistakable and brighten up the roadsides. But its beauty is deceiving, as it will rob all nutrients for years from the soil around it. The seeds are most often spread by the wind and animals moving through the brush.

Control at this point is difficult and most communities have gone to concerted efforts to eradicate these weeds. Pulling out by the roots is most effective, and certainly this should be done before the flowers set seed in mid-spring. But this is also a labor-intensive, difficult way to control it. Spraying large areas is generally ineffective, and I have also heard of landowners burning off a field, a dangerous project, as the oils in the plant burn readily and its presence is considered to be a fire hazard. So, labor-intensive or not, the best thing to do is to pull it out whenever you see it creeping into your garden. Start with the smallest plants before they grow too tall to manage and be diligent in getting out the roots.

Gorse is a similar plant as are Spanish, Portuguese, and French broom, and although they are from different botanical families, control is pretty much the same as for the Scotch broom. Remove them all and avoid planting them in your gardens.

Giant Horsetail

Giant horsetail (*Equisetum arvense*) has mysteriously escaped most of the noxious weeds lists. At the present time, I have only found it on Oregon's list. But perhaps this is because it is considered to be a native plant, and thus, technically, not "noxious," a term that seems to be reserved for imported plants. But if there has ever been a noxious plant, this is it. It has several stages of growth, starting as an asparagus-looking sprout that soon enough "blossoms" into a feathery, brushlike shape. Thus the name "horsetail," or *Equisetum*, as it is said to look like a horse's tail. But it also has creeping roots that will soon form a mat of weeds that will crowd any desirable plants out of the garden.

There are million-year-old fossils of this plant, so I count on it being difficult to eradicate. I really only get upset with this plant when it comes close to my gardens, as it is attractive when growing in the wild where it belongs. If it behaves itself and stays along the roadsides and in the native forests, I will leave it alone. When I find it in the neighbors' yards, I try to firmly but gently pull it out by the roots before it spreads into my gardens. In my own (or in clients' gardens) I will spray to remove it. Persistence is needed and I have found using glyphosate in the

Equisetum (Giant Horsetail) as first sprouting

early fall is most effective. This is when the *Equisetum* nutrients are moving from its leaves back into the roots, and they will take the poison with them. But because horsetails grow among other desirable plants, I need to use an eye dropper or small paint brush to apply glyphosate to the weed, and I am very careful not to apply the chemical on windy days when the drift might escape and effect the perennials.

Canadian Thistle (Cirsium arvense)

An aggressive plant that has made almost all of the coastal weed lists is the Canadian thistle. As it was most likely introduced from Eurasia, it isn't even Canadian, nor is it wanted in Canada. The female and male flowers are on separate plants. The purple flowers sit on top of heads that are the least spiny of the thistle family, and it also has spiny wings along thin stems. The deep, creeping rhizomes make this plant difficult to eradicate, and it becomes very problematic when it takes hold in pasture lands. The best way to control this plant is to persistently cut it back low to the ground. You will eventually weaken the plant until it dies.

Himalayan Blackberry (Rubus procerus*)*

Another introduced problem for coastal gardeners has been the Himalayan blackberry. When ripe, the berries are sweet and delicious and can be used for pies, jams, and eating fresh. However, the plant's spiny, thorned branches are weak but may grow erect or in a rambling, thick mat that will smother plants around it. There is also an evergreen blackberry *(Rubus laciniatus)* that, although less aggressive, is a noxious weed as well. Although both have white flowers and purple berries, the evergreen plants are distinguished from the Himalayan by their deeply but irregularly toothed and incised leaves. Repeated cutting to the ground of these plants will, over time, weaken them. If you are pulling them out, be sure to remove the root crowns or the plants will regenerate. Several applications of glyphosate in the fall will be necessary if you are trying to use chemicals to kill them. Again, be careful of harming surrounding desirable plants. You may want to leave a bush or two for the fruit, but be diligent about keeping them under control.

Japanese Knotweed (Polygonum cuspidatum*)*

A bully in the riparian areas of the Pacific Northwest is the imported Japanese knotweed. It can easily grow to six feet or more in dense, shrublike thickets. The leaves are large (up to six inches) and are ovate with an abrupt pointed tip. The small white-to-green flowers are grouped in clusters close to the ends of the stems. In a large plot, they can be beautiful and were no doubt imported as a garden plant. It spreads most rapidly in moist places and is most problematic near stream beds. Repeated cutting seems to have little effect and may even cause a further growth spurt. The home gardener may find spraying shortly after the plant blooms to be the most effective control. However, since this plant grows close to water sources, it is best to check with your local extension agent as to the approved chemical to use for your situation. It may have to be applied by a registered pesticide technician. Other members of this weed family include common knotweed (*Polygonum aviculare*), beach knotweed (*Polygonum paronychia*), and giant knotweed (*Polygonim sachalinense*).

Creeping Red Wood Sorrel (Oxalis corniculata)

This small but aggressive perennial weed is the scourge of many coastal gardeners. It can often be found in pots from the nursery, so be certain to remove it from around the roots of your new plants before you place them in the ground. Red wood sorrel has a prostrate growing habit, and the leaves are shaped like a clover but are generally a reddish purple. The flowers are small and yellow and bloom several times during the year. This is a creeping plant, with stolons that root at the nodes and run just under the soil, helping the wood sorrel to increase its numbers. Once established in your gardens, it is very difficult to eradicate, mostly because it hides under desirable perennials and annuals. Spraying with a broadleaf weed killer is thus not effective. The best thing to do is to weed it out as soon as you see it, certainly before the flowers go to seed or it becomes even more invasive. Try to collect as much of the runners as possible. Do not compost this weed.

Giant Hogweed (Heracleum mantegazzianum)

Giant hogweed can be a different kind of problem for northwestern gardeners. It is found along stream banks but also in moist slopes and

Creeping red wood sorrel

clearings as well as upper beaches and dunes. It is common from sea level to the mountains. This is a huge plant, growing to 10 or 12 feet high in the right conditions. A member of the carrot family and relative to Queen Anne's lace and cow parsnip, the giant hogweed can cause severe dermatitis and enduring blisters once the plant has been touched and then the skin exposed to the sun.

Control of giant hogweed consists of proper timing of applications of glyphosate. By applying at the bud stage when the plant is actively growing, you will have more success. But even glyphosate has limited effectiveness and will have to be reapplied. The alternative to using chemicals is to dig out the entire root stalk. But be certain to wear protective clothing on your legs, arms, hands, and feet because of the potential of dermatitis when working with any portion of this plant.

Dandelion (Taraxacum officinale)

While not on the noxious weed list, the common dandelion will no doubt be the bane of many coastal gardeners. There are actually two forms of dandelion, and until recently the false dandelion (Hypochaeris radicata) was the only dandelion-type weed we needed to deal with. However, the eastern version has slowly crept westward and can now be found in many coastal—as well as inland—areas. The best part about the false dandelion is that it was easier to pull than its more tenacious eastern cousin. Both have entirely basal leaves, meaning they are close to the ground. The common dandelion, however, generally has only one flower and flower-stem per plant. The false dandelion usually has more than one flower head. The flowers are yellow in both cases and produce airy seed heads that disperse easily in the winds.

The best control is to pull the dandelions from the gardens and lawns as you see them. I use a forked digger and pry as much of the root as possible, or the root will regrow. If your lawn is infested, it may be best to spray with an herbicide registered for use on broad-leaved weeds. Again keep in mind that most perennials and annuals are considered to be broad-leaved plants as well and will be killed more easily than the dandelions should the chemical spray stray.

Yellow Star Thistle (Centaurea solstitialis)

This annual weed is a member of the knapweed/sunflower family and is found on all the western states' noxious weeds lists. But since this is a plant that prefers dry grasslands, it has not yet adapted to the moist Pacific Northwest coastal climate. Be aware of it, however, and do not import it, even by accident, to the coastal areas as "hitchhikers" with plants purchased inland. It has dandelion-yellow flowers atop a tube with very spiny spikes that make dealing with this plant painful.

Tansy Ragwort (Senecio jacobaea)

This noxious weed is currently making inroads on the Oregon and Washington coasts, especially in pastureland, where this poisonous plant affects livestock. Another member of the sunflower family, it is a short-lived perennial that can grow up to three feet. It has a long tap-root that is difficult—but necessary—to remove. The multiple bright-yellow flower heads sit atop the stems in a flat-topped manner, and each head is about an inch across. Because of its invasive tendencies, environmentalists are importing Japanese flea beetles and the Cinnabar moth caterpillar to help in the fight against this European native.

Leafy Spurge (Euphorbia esula) and
Petty Spurge (Euphorbia peplus)

While leafy spurge is considered a noxious weed in many Pacific Northwest states, we are not as bothered with it on the coast as we are its close cousin petty spurge. Neither should be confused with the lovely garden plant family of euphorbias, however, although they are similar in growing habit and leaf form. Petty spurge is often found in gardens on the coast and, if pulled before going to flower, is easily removed. Petty spurge is an annual weed, while leafy spurge is a perennial. Both have the euphorbias' characteristic of having a milky sap that can be caustic to the skin, mouth, and eyes. This family includes the poinsettia, and several other ornamental plants, some of which are more toxic than others. Wear gloves when weeding this plant from the flower beds, and wash your hands and arms carefully, avoiding eye and mouth contact.

Sheep Sorrel (Rumex acetosella)

Sheep sorrel is a common garden weed in the northwest and since it has creeping rhizomes can be difficult to remove. The leaves are mostly basal and are shaped like a narrow arrowhead. Found in the wild on disturbed sites, it can be invasive in a garden if left unattended. Introduced from Europe, it spreads by seeds and rather delicate rhizomes that break easily when pulled and will just as easily resprout. The name sorrel comes from the French *surelle*, meaning sour, because of the acidity of the leaves. Best to be persistent with this one, but use a light hand in pulling out as much of the rhizome as you can. Fortunately, the garden variety is not generally deeply rooted and if the soil is moist, a gentle lifting can often remove a long strand of the root.

Hedge and Field Bindweed

These two weeds are closely related to the morning glory family and are considered to be perennial weeds. Field bindweed (*Convolvulous arvensis*) is a problem in pastures, but hedge bindweed (*Convolvulus sepium*) is the weed that will most likely invade your garden. Both grow from rhizomes that go deep underground, making them hard to remove. They twine around plants and if left to grow, will choke and smother the life from them. The morning glory–like flowers are usually white and resemble trumpets. Try to pull them before the flowers go to seed or these invasive plants will reproduce even faster. These annual vines will die back at the first sign of cold weather, but their roots are deep enough underground that they will send up new shoots when the rains stop and the earth warms in the spring. This is the best time to control this weed and persistence in pulling the sprouts will eventually weaken the plants and they will die. Chemical control is difficult as it generally should be applied just after blooming, which means other plants are also at risk from the chemicals.

Little Western Bittercress (Cardamine oligosperma)

The bittercresses have basal leaves consisting of deeply divided lobes where the larger lobe is at the end of the leaf. These form a

Bindweed

rosette that makes it easy to identify this annual garden pest. This annual or biennial weed forms a very pretty little white flower at the ends of taller, branched leaves. When this plant goes to seed, if it is in any way disturbed, the tiny seeds will scatter in a spray. While listed officially as an annual weed, the temperatures on the coast are mild enough to insure year-round seeding and growth so—once again— persistence is necessary. Watch for this pest all year in your garden and pull it as you find it. It is easily pulled from the soil, but will also hide under perennial plants. Best control for this pest is to hand weed it out as soon as you see the basal leaves and certainly before it flowers or goes to seed.

*Fireweed (*Epilobium angustifolium*)*

Usually found along the roadsides of the inland areas in the northwest, this weed is slowly but surely creeping toward the coast. It holds wildflower status in some states and is very pretty when seen along the road in large numbers, less pretty when invading the garden. A tall perennial, fireweed has lance-shaped leaves without a noticeable stalk. The flowers range from rose to purple in long clusters along the top of the stems. This weed likes moist as well as dry areas and is usually found only in certain locations along the coastal areas.

Cardamine oligosperma (Little Bittercress)

*Purple-Leaved Willow Herb (*Epilobium ciliatum*)*

A relative of fireweed, the smaller purple-leaved willow herb is rather a pretty weed, but can get out of hand easily, making it another garden pest. It is considered to be a perennial and has small bulblike rhizomes. The growth habit is erect and it can grow to 12 inches tall in the garden. The leaves are opposite and long oval in form. The flowers can be white, purple, or rose and are arrayed on the top of the stem in clusters. This weed prefers moist soils so it is found commonly in coastal gardens. The purple-leaved willow herb spreads by seeds, so control before the flowers go to seed is necessary. Happily, it is easily pulled from the garden.

DISEASES

A disease may be defined as a disorder that is detrimental to health. In the case of plant diseases, it may not only be detrimental to the plants, but also have an effect on the value of the plant, flower, or crop. While many plant diseases are prevalent on the coast, most of them are fungal because of the moist, cool conditions with little or no freezing, but there are also viral and bacterial diseases that will affect coastal plants. By being aware of the possibilities and symptoms of each of these diseases that may affect our gardens, we can be on the lookout for them and get a jump on protecting our plants before the disease affects them adversely. Some diseases are more cosmetic than lethal, and a gardener needs to decide her or his tolerance level for the scarring but not deadly blemishes on the plants.

There are two types of diseases, whether we are talking about the animal kingdom or the plant kingdom: *infectious* and *noninfectious*. When we talk about human diseases, measles is an example of infectious, while heart disease is noninfectious. If we are talking about plants, most of the fungal diseases are infectious and can be passed not only from one part of the plant to another, but also from plant to plant. An example of a noninfectious plant disease is a gall.

The many living organisms that can cause a disease are called *pathogens*. Most are microscopic and difficult to see without magnification. So we need to be aware of the symptoms in order to diagnose our problem. Fungi come in many forms and reproduce by spores. They are able to manufacture toxins that will kill plant cells or will grow within the plant or its roots and interrupt the ability for the plant to produce or utilize nutrients.

Viral organisms are the smallest of the pathogens and so are more difficult to identify, except with electron microscopes. Viruses do tend to produce unusual patterns, plant colors, or plant forms. They can also infect seeds and tubers and affect generations of plants. Not all viruses are toxic to the plant and some are encouraged by plant breeders and growers. For example, a tulip's fantastic coloration and streaks are often caused by viral infections that cause the "sports" and will be genetically passed to future generations.

While bacteria and nematodes are not as prevalent in our coastal diseases, they are, at times, factors. Bacteria can build to high enough numbers that they ooze out of the plant tissue and can attract insects to the weakened plant. These insects help to spread the bacteria to other plants as the insects move through the garden. Bacteria break down the cell walls by forming enzymes or toxins. Nematodes—microscopic roundworms—can be vectors of plant diseases, passing them from plant to plant. They may move from root to root or attack foliage.

As we discussed in chapter 5, in order for a plant to become infected with a disease, three factors need to be present. The first is the host plant that is susceptible to the pathogen—not all plants are affected by any one disease. The second factor is that the pathogen itself must be present as an active, living bacteria, fungi, or virus. The third factor in a disease infection is that the environment must be favorable for the pathogen to grow. If the weather is too hot, too cold, too rainy, or too dry, a specific disease will not take hold. If we remove any of these factors—host plant, pathogen or environment—a disease will not be able to occur.

We also need to become familiar with the insects that can affect our plants. Some insect damage mimics that of a disease and we want to avoid treating for disease if the problem is a pest, and vice versa.

The cycle of disease is important to know for treating or controlling the pathogen. Knowing when the disease is at its weakest point in its life cycle and knowing how and when a pathogen reproduces will enlighten you to the best time to attack. Many pathogens do not actively cause disease during the adverse conditions of winter. Several canker diseases will have only one life cycle per year. Powdery mildew, however, is an example of a disease that will reproduce in many cycles during the growing season. Being aware of these cycles will help us diagnose and control infections.

We can also interrupt a disease infection by knowing when, where, and what to plant. Planting at the proper time of year can aid the plant in staying healthy and pathogen-free. Some diseases are soil-borne and will remain in the soil for many years. Planting in these diseased areas will only insure frustration as subsequent plants fall prey to the same pathogens. Remember our crop rotation. Many plants are being bred now to be disease resistant for certain pathogens. But disease resistant means just that: resistant, not immune.

Diagnosing Plant Diseases

There are several questions to ask yourself when trying to diagnose a plant problem. The first, and most important, is to know what kind of plant you have and what is considered "normal" for that species. The plant's age, size, and location in relation to other plants; weather; and soil conditions are also important to evaluate. Look for symptoms of a disease such as cankers, wilting, rotting, chlorosis (yellowing of leaves not normally yellow), and galls. These can be described as the physical disease characteristics of the plant. But also look for signs that are the physical evidence of a pathogen being present (like fungal spores or bacterial slime) or chemical residues and insect webs. Signs would also include indications of weather-related damage, for example, hailstones on the ground, or a notation in your garden journal of extremely high winds just before damage was noticed.

Disease Control Principles

There are five principles of disease control. The first is *exclusion*. Exclusion is a technique that prevents diseased plant materials from moving into an area. Careful inspections of the plants you purchase from anyone is the first line of defense. State and local governments may also issue quarantines. Diseases such as filbert blight, azalea flower spot, and Sudden Oak Death are examples of disease quarantines imposed by the states.

Avoidance is the second step in disease control. A disease that has already been brought into your region may be avoided by planting in the proper spot at the proper time of the season. Planting certified virus-free plants is another means of avoidance. The *Phytophthora* root rots can be avoided by planting in well-drained soil. Keep from wounding a plant when placing it in the ground. Wounds are perfect spots for pathogens that may weaken the plant. Use proper pruning techniques as well as watering, fertilizing, and training methods to keep the plants healthy. A healthy plant is more likely to be able to fight off disease.

The third step in control is *eradication*. Crop rotation, good sanitation of the planted area throughout the year and elimination of alternate hosts are several ways of eradicating a disease. Using certain chemicals can also eliminate pathogens. And sterilizing our tools is a good habit when working in the garden as well.

Another possible step in disease management is *protection*. If we know a disease is in the area, we may choose to treat our healthy plants before they become infected. By starting treatment before the pathogen reaches the plant, we are setting up a defense so the plant has added protection against the disease when it does arrive. Chemicals such as fungicides set up a protective coating on the foliage of the plant. Keep in mind that frequent reapplication may be necessary during rainy or windy weather. Fungicides registered for home use are less toxic than those available to certified technicians and is another reason they will need to be reapplied.

The fifth control in disease management is *resistance*, using plant varieties that have been bred to be resistant to certain diseases. Plant catalogs and seed companies will most likely note if a plant is disease resistant as it is a big selling point for many species. Hybrid tea roses are a good example. Many are dreadfully susceptible to the fungal diseases of black spot and rust, but most rose growers are trying to breed bushes that are at least tolerant if not resistant to black spot. Of course on the coast, our black spot is very tenacious and even a resistant cultivar may find itself looking rather spotty by mid-August. This is especially true in a cool, damp summer. During a dry summer, black spot is less of a problem, because, as I mentioned earlier, the fungal disease needs the proper environment for reproduction.

If a plant is never susceptible to a disease it can be considered to be immune. Tolerance is another level of susceptibility and means the plant may contract the disease but will grow in a normal way.

Discouraging Diseases

Here are some ideas for deterring diseases. Not all will work, of course, but by using as many as possible it will reduce the likelihood of disease problems.

- Choose the proper location for the plant. If the plant prefers sun, plant it in the sun. Shade-loving plants should be in the shade. By picking the proper location, you will allow the plant to grow more robust and thus give it more of a chance if a disease does strike. Steer clear of planting in cool, damp soil because those conditions are perfect for many root-borne diseases. If you have an area of cool, wet soil, choose only the proper plant for the site.
- Rotate the vegetables and annuals every year and avoid replanting in the same area on a three year cycle. This will not only help prevent the buildup of disease organisms, it will help with insect control.
- If available, select disease-resistant varieties of plants that are good for your location.

- Buy only disease-free seed, soil, and transplants. Inspect all plants carefully. When buying seeds, look for ones that are certified disease-free. Buy from reputable nurseries who take pride in their stock. If a plant is growing poorly, dig it out and throw it away.
- Do not compost diseased plants. Period.
- By using proper fertilizer and soil amendments, you can maintain a healthy pH for the plants you are growing. A proper pH means a vigorous, healthy plant. Do not over- or underfertilize. Read the directions on the container and follow them closely.
- Avoid overcrowding your plants. Yes, it may look nicer to have a lush, full border of perennials, but if they are too close the air can not circulate and the soil will harbor fungal diseases. Keep in mind the mature size of perennials, trees, shrubs, and grasses before putting them in the ground.
- Take a walk in your gardens every day and look at the plants thoroughly. Watch for signs of insects that may weaken the plant or spread viral or bacterial diseases. Be alert for the symptoms and signs of problems and address them promptly.
- Be aware of disease cycles and know when to look for them during the year. Some diseases occur yearly on certain plants. By being vigilant you will see the problems as they begin to occur and can act on them before they spread.
- Water only when necessary and then in the morning so the foliage has time to dry before nightfall. Try to avoid fluctuations of very dry to very wet and maintain an even water supply to the plants. If possible, group plants according to watering needs as well as light conditions to make for ease of watering. Drip irrigation and soaker hoses are usually more efficient than overhead watering or watering by hand. Most plants need their roots watered, not their leaves.
- At the first sign of disease, remove affected plants. Place them in the garbage rather than the compost pile to avoid spreading the pathogens in the compost. Some sources say composting of diseased material is okay if you are "hot" composting, but some pathogens are not killed even in high temperatures, so it's easier to just not "recycle" problems.

There are many good diagnostic books that can help you discover what problem is affecting your plants. For simplicity's sake, choose one that has good photographs of the host plants and shows how they are affected by the diseases.

Coastal Diseases

Following are some of the most common and problematic of the coastal diseases. Once again, the controls available will differ from state to state or province, so it is best to check with your local extension office for chemical recommendations that are legal in your area.

Verticillium Wilt (*Verticillium dahliae*): These fungal bodies live in the soil and also in diseased plants. Once established in the soil, they are very difficult to eradicate. The fungus infects the vascular system of the plants, which makes it difficult for the plant to move nutrients from the roots into the leaves. It affects many trees such as redbuds, ash, box elders, maples, and smoke trees. Also affected are roses, viburnum, heathers, fuchsias and lilacs, asters, dahlias, geraniums, peonies, blackberries, raspberries, cabbage, cucumbers, peppers, potatoes, tomatoes, and pumpkins. Each plant displays different symptoms, but generally the plant will show signs of stress and will begin to wilt from the bottom up. The lower leaves will turn yellow and fall as the wilt works its way up the plant. Remove the infected plants and dispose of them in the garbage. The fungal bodies will remain in the soil for several years, so avoid planting any other type of susceptible plant in the same location. Disinfect all tools once you are done using them to avoid spreading the soilborne particles to other areas of the garden. Some breeders are developing disease-resistant cultivars and these should be searched for and used.

Anthracnose: Anthracnose is another group of fungal bodies that affect coastal plants such as maples, tomatoes, apple trees, blackberries, peppers, raspberries, and lawns. Different species attack different plants, but in general, they love the damp climate in the northwest. They also thrive in the high humidity that sometimes occurs when spring temperatures warm rapidly.

In trees, the fungal bodies spend the winter on fallen leaves, and when the spring rains come, the spores are splashed onto newly forming young leaves. They may also overwinter in cankers or lesions that develop on the trees' bark. In a very rainy season, the spots will expand on the leaves, eventually covering them and killing them, causing premature defoliation. If this defoliation occurs early enough in the year, the tree may recover and grow new leaves. If the infection is allowed to continue for several years, the branches will be affected and killed as well.

On fruits, the anthracnose will cause small, sunken, circular spots on the fruit that will merge and infect the entire fruit. This is especially true for tomatoes. It is most commonly found on overripe fruit, and fruit that is low to the ground. It renders the tomatoes inedible.

To avoid anthracnose on tomatoes, pick the fruit as it ripens and use them promptly. Avoid working around wet plants to keep from spreading the disease. Do not use overhead irrigation and do not overwater. Stake the tomatoes to keep them off the ground. After the tomatoes have been harvested, clean up debris and destroy it promptly. Rotate the tomato crops on at least a three-year rotation.

In the case of trees, a single year's infection will generally not harm the tree. But rake and burn any fallen leaves promptly. During dormancy, prune out any dead twigs, especially ones with cankers. If the following spring is also rainy and humid, you may need to resort to a fungicide application when the leaves begin to uncurl.

Anthracnose in turf has two phases. The first is active in the summer and causes yellow or brown lesions on the older grass leaves. The second phase is the basal stem rot that is found in the fall and winter on the coast. The old leaves will begin to turn yellow at the tips and change to a bright orange. Patches are generally small. To avoid anthracnose becoming a problem in the lawn, water the grass thoroughly but only when needed. Remove any thatch and aerate the lawn on a regular basis. Maintain a healthy nutrient program for the lawn and mow higher in periods of stress such as hot, dry weather.

Phytophthora Root Rots: This group of root rot fungi species is dependent on the plants involved. For example, one type of phytophthora will attack raspberries, while another will attack rhododendrons and azaleas, and yet another will attack peppers and eggplants. Several plants, like true fir trees, are unlucky enough to be susceptible to several of the phytophthoras.

Phytophthora fungi are more commonly referred to as "water molds," which indicates the conditions in which they grow: in water, in saturated soil, along ponds and riverbanks, and in flood-prone areas. Because of the high rainfall amounts in the Pacific Northwest, several phytophthora species thrive here.

The symptoms to look for when diagnosing phytophthora involves inspection of the roots of the plant as well as the tops. Diagnosing solely from the top of the plant is ineffective as many diseases or problems mimic symptoms of the water molds. Wilting, chlorosis (yellowing of the leaves), and premature leaf-fall can be symptomatic of anything that girdles the plants to cut off water and nutrient supply. These may also be indications of root weevil larvae, winter injury, or lack of water. So the symptoms of root involvement are best explored. This, of course, will mean digging it up. When you do, look to see if the plant has few feeder roots with remaining roots dark or in stages of decay. The root tips will show the most severe effects and the root crown will show the least. Use a small knife to cut and expose the vascular cambium of the root. If phytophthora is active, you will see a discolored area between the bark (phloem) and the inner wood (xylem). The distinction between a healthy area and a diseased one will generally be a sharp margin. The water molds generally start low on the plant and work their way upward, but this is not the case for all plants. In some cases, a sample of the roots will have to be sent to a laboratory for analysis of the plant to confirm a diagnosis and pinpoint a specific phytophthora species.

The best way to control these fungi is to stop them before they start infecting your plants. Regulate water to the plants with irrigation methods. Insure proper drainage by using well-drained soil. In the case of container plantings, tilt the container and provide adequate drainage holes. Use clean, disease-free nursery stock; use disease-resistant varieties; rotate your crops. Use raised beds or mounds. For example, for raspberries, mound up the soil before planting to allow for additional drainage. Use clean or sterile soil. Once the molds are present they are harder to eradicate. Some areas have found success in using copper-based fungicides. Other chemicals usually must be professionally applied, so unless it is affecting many species, removal of the infected plants may be preferable. Replace them with plants that are not susceptible to any of the phytophthora rots.

Late Blight (*Phytophthora infestans*): Late blight is prevalent on the coast, as it thrives in cool, damp weather. It affects tomatoes and potatoes but only a few other related plants such as eggplants and peppers. The lesions begin on the plant as irregular, greenish, water-soaked spots on any part of the plant. The spots will enlarge quickly to form dark, almost black, purple lesions. In areas with extreme dampness, a white mold may also appear on the lower leaf edges. Rainy weather, high dew amounts, and fog will all help this disease to spread. It dislikes hot, dry weather but can be harbored in infected stems to await the return of dampness. Normally this fungus does not survive in the soil or on the dead plant debris, but infected tomato and potato refuse should be removed and bagged for disposal. This includes any volunteer plants, even in the compost pile. Crop rotation is important to avoid this problem in subsequent years. Usually the disease will overwinter in potato tubers, or be brought in on seeds or transplants, which is less likely because of commercial growers being so careful to avoid diseased products. Buy from a reputable grower and look for plants free of symptoms. When watering, avoid getting the foliage wet, and water early in the day so the plants can dry off before nightfall. Stake tomatoes and allow lots of room between plants for good air circulation. Look for disease-resistant varieties. And rotate those crops!

Early Blight (*Alternaria tomatophilai*): Early blight is another disease that can affect tomato and potato relatives. This fungus is able to overwinter in the soil, and it prefers high humidity, temperatures between 75 to 85 degrees, and low soil fertility. Older leaves will show symptoms first, with small but irregular black-brown spots. The spots will enlarge and show rings in a pattern that resembles a target. Leaf tissue around the spots will turn yellow, but the greatest injury is to the fruits as they begin to ripen. Again, the best way to avoid this disease is to rotate the crops in at least a three-year pattern. Start with disease-free seeds or transplants and maintain healthy plants with fertilization and proper irrigation. Destroy any plant debris after harvest.

Black Spot (*Diplocarpon rosae*): Black spot is the common term for a fungal disease that is prevalent on coastal as well as inland roses. The disease is named for its symptoms—black spots on the leaves or, more rarely, the flowers or stems of a plant. The spots start small and increase in size. They are generally circular with a fringed edge. The tissue around the spot may turn yellow as the disease progresses, and the leaves may prematurely drop from the bush. Plants that are severely affected may lose all their leaves and the flower numbers are reduced and of poor quality. Plants that are repeatedly affected over several years may be unable to fight the disease and will die.

Spraying with an approved fungicide at the first sign of a problem is generally the best method of control. The spraying may have to be repeated as often as every week or two as long as the weather stays cool and damp. Allowing good air circulation between plants, having good sanitation practices, and avoiding overhead watering are some ways to prevent the disease. But accept the fact that no matter what you do, if you live on the Pacific Northwest coast, your roses may be infected again each year. Be sure to collect all the fallen leaves around the base of the plant as they fall and burn them. Prune off any affected rose canes. When the new growth starts the following spring, start spraying as soon as new shoots appear.

Choosing rose varieties that are resistant to black spot and applying a systemic rose food/fungicide may also help to alleviate the problem.

Powdery Mildew (*Sphaerotheca pannosa var. rosae*): Powdery mildew is another fungal disease that affects roses and can be one of the most serious diseases that roses contract. The roses' young twigs, buds, and leaves appear to be covered with a thin, white powder. Once infected, the leaves may curl and be distorted, then turn a purple color and drop off. New growth is often stunted and new canes may be killed in a severe infestation. Buds will also become distorted before opening. In the fall, a light coating of tiny pepper-like black spots will be dotted over the powder. These are the spore-producing bodies.

Wind helps to disperse this disease to healthy plants, so spacing between plants is recommended. Powdery mildew prefers drier, warmer conditions with low daytime and higher nighttime humidity. Therefore, on the coast, control may not be necessary until later in the summer when the weather tends to dry out.

Again, planting disease-resistant varieties is your best bet, along with maintaining good sanitation of fallen leaves. Several chemical treatments are approved for use by homeowners as well. Some chemicals combine control of both black spot and powdery mildew in the same application.

Rust (*Phragmidium species*): Rust is another group of rose fungal diseases that affects northwest bushes. It appears as orange spots on the leaves, usually on the lower surface, with brown and yellow spots on the upper surfaces. The lower orange spots can generally be scraped off, but this doesn't mean the disease is not present once the orange spots are removed. The disease is most evident in the spring or late fall. Wind will spread the orange fungal spores from plant to plant. When the weather stays moist with rain, dew, or even fog and the temperatures remain moderate (55 to 75 degrees), the spores are able to infect the tissues on the lower sides of the leaves. The yellow or brown spots appear directly above them on the upper surface. When autumn arrives and the weather cools further, the upper spots will become black spores and will winter on the leaf. In the spring the spores will become active once again and move from plant to plant in the wind, causing new infections. Twigs may become infected and the plants' health and vigor will be reduced.

To control rust, pick off and destroy any leaves at the first sign of the orange spots. Rake and destroy any leaves from the ground in addition to pruning any infected twigs or canes from the rose. An approved fungicide may need to be used every week to 10 days for best control.

Hosta Virus X: Hosta Virus X (also known as HVX) showed up about five years ago when mottled leaves were appearing on some hostas. Interestingly, the growers did not recognize it as a virus and thought it was a new variety. Some plants were even named and sold as newly discovered hostas. By the time the breeders realized it was a disease and not a new plant, the virus was already spreading. Some of the "breeds" that are actually infected plants are 'Breakdance', 'Leopard Frog', and 'Lunacy'.

The symptoms that you should look for vary with the cultivar. On light-colored leaves, look for dark green or bluish veins that resemble "bleeding" as ink will do on a porous surface. On darker leaves, the virus causes a yellowish, mottled look. Even though a plant is not in strong sunlight, it may have a bleached or spotty look.

A few varieties have been more affected than others. These include the very popular 'Sum and Substance', 'Gold Standard', and 'Striptease'.

In fact, the virus on 'Striptease' is difficult to diagnose as the mottling may look like part of this plant's variegation patterns. Another problem with HVX is that an infected plant might not show signs of disease for several years. In 'Sum and Substance', the plants may take up to seven years to display symptoms.

HVX is also very easily spread to other, healthy hostas, primarily by the sap that is released when a plant is cut. Dividing hostas, removing blooms or leaves, accidentally stepping on them, or cutting them with a lawn mower can discharge the pathogen onto the cutting tool or even the bottom of your garden boot. Even the flowers and roots carry infected sap.

Fortunately, HVX only survives in a living plant and will die without contact with a host hosta. It will not live in the soil to reinfect any subsequent hostas planted there. That's the good news.

We must be conscientious about our gardening cleanliness. This means disinfecting our tools, hands, gloves, and even our boots after working with our hostas. Clean your pruners after working with each plant using a bleach and water solution. This is necessary when deadheading, cutting, or transplanting hostas. If you suspect a plant has been affected, dig it up immediately and place it in a bag for the garbage. Get every root and each bit of living tissue. Do not compost it. Do not place it in your brush pile. Sterilize your shovel with the bleach/water mix. Clean your hands thoroughly as well as your tools and gloves. I cannot stress this enough. Simply touching a healthy plant when the sap is on your glove can infect that new hosta.

When you are shopping for hostas, be especially careful not to purchase a diseased plant, no matter how great that new variegation may look in your yard. Pass it by. Deal with reputable nurserymen. And if you see a plant in the nursery that is showing these symptoms, please tell someone at the garden center. There are laboratory tests available for growers to have their plants tested. Most growers are already aware of this problem and are taking steps to eliminate stock that has been infected.

Sudden Oak Death (*Phytophthora ramorum*): Sudden Oak Death is a water mold that causes two types of diseases, one of which may kill the host with bark cancers and the other that causes leaf blights that harbor the pathogens and serve as agents for the spread of the molds. There is no known cure for Sudden Oak Death, and it affects nursery-grown rhododendrons, camellias, azaleas, and viburnums as well as oaks, big leaf maples, and Douglas fir. Buy from a certified grower in your state who is aware of the problem and has taken steps to address it in his stock. Never buy a plant that looks stressed or diseased. Sudden

Oak Death symptoms include droplets of dark red-brown liquid seeping from a bark canker that girdles the tree or shrub. Foliar hosts have lesions that are dark gray to brown with indistinct edges anywhere on the leaf blade or in the vascular tissue of the leave or its stem.

Remove infected plants and destroy them. Do not compost them.

INSECTS

More than one million insect species have been identified in the world, and over 90,000 of them live in North America. The largest number of species exist in the beetle, fly, moth/butterfly, and wasp/ant/bee orders. But in all those insects, less than one percent are serious pests for humans, animals, and crops. The insects that are problems, however, can be very destructive toward agricultural crops, do severe structural damage, and be transporters of disease-causing pathogens.

Luckily for all of humanity, most insects are relatively harmless and in some cases are beneficial. Some are predators of harmful insects, some are pollinating vectors, and many types of insects help to break down animal and plant matter and aid in its decay. Some insects can be good in one aspect but harmful in another. Obviously termites are good to help the decaying process in the forest when the trees fall, but they will be trouble when they cross the paths of humans living in wooden homes.

Insects vary in size and appearance. They vary in the way they chew and digest their food. They vary in how and when they breed. But all insects have three body parts: head, thorax, and abdomen. They are grouped into eight "orders" according to these parts, the type of legs, and style of wings, if there are any. And identification of an insect and the placing of it in its proper order can be useful in determining how much of a pest it can be and how to control populations. Knowing the group to which an insect belongs will help in identifying the damage that can be done. Look for telltale signs of trails, chewing patterns, and frass (insect "droppings") to help with the identification. Also, knowing the host plant will be important because many insects are plant specific. Aphids, for example, prefer plants with high nitrogen content like roses. If you find tissue loss in a plant, it is generally damage done by an insect with chewing mouthparts.

In many cases, as a gardener, it is difficult to identify which insect is causing a problem unless you actually see it eating the plant. Just the presence of an insect on a chewed leaf does not always mean it is that particular insect that was doing the chewing. Catching the true culprit in the act, however, is tricky and in many cases impossible unless you are willing to sit and watch a plant for long periods of time, day and night.

There are many good books to help you identify insects with drawings or photographs. A good reference guide that you can take into the garden will no doubt be helpful. A list of suggested material is included in the Reference Guide at the back of this book. As a serious gardener, it might be helpful to invest in an identification loupe. This small magnifying glass can be slipped into your gardening bucket or put on a lanyard and worn around your neck. They cost about $10 and are generally found in stores selling scientific items or in university bookstores.

The field of entomology can be studied for years, obviously, and as there are so many kinds of insects, we will limit our discussion to ones that have been known to affect coastal gardens. I will not give any chemical recommendations for insect control, as insecticides are regulated by each state and what is legal in California or Washington may not be approved for use in Oregon. This is another case where you should check with your county extension agent to see what you can legally use as a homeowner. In severe cases, a professional exterminator may need to be called in to assess and address the problem. You also need to decide for yourself what your level of tolerance will be. Termites and carpenter ants, of course, should be at a level of zero tolerance, but if you only have a few box elder bugs and you can keep them from invading your home, you may find their presence a nonissue. I would advise using chemical controls only when you are unable to control the problem with other, less toxic means.

Slugs and Snails

These pests are the ones that Pacific Northwest gardeners complain about the most, and they aren't even insects, but mollusks. There are about 40 species of slugs in the Pacific Northwest, and many are quite large and can do considerable damage to hostas, vegetables, dahlias, and other ornamental plants. They prefer dining at night because they like cool, dark spaces. Interestingly, they move to the dark when its light and toward the light when its dark, which is why you will find them around lit areas of the garden at night. They have favorite kinds of plants, but they also will eat just about anything if hungry enough. For every 5 you see, there are 95 you don't. Slugs can burrow into small cracks in the ground and can literally "spread themselves thin," up to 11 times their normal length to fit into small spaces.

Snails are a bit different and are more limited to where they can go because of their shells. But they, too, can be voracious pests in the garden. There are only a few native snails in the Pacific Northwest and they prefer the forested areas. But several species of snails are moving into the area from other parts of the country and indeed, the world, in pots or under tiles that have been imported from as far away as the Mediterranean.

Baits are most effective, and the location of the baits' placement is important. Most baits have a chemical called metaldehyde, or "meta," in them as well as an attractant. The slugs or snails will be drawn to the attractant but may become distracted and eat the plant before going to the bait. And metaldehyde only stuns their system. Usually the slug will be paralyzed and dry out in the sun. But if the bait is placed around, say, hostas, the shade will shelter the slug until the chemical wears off. A better idea is to place the slug bait near where they spend the day: cool, dark areas under ground covers, near rock walls, under boards or other garden debris, and not around your favorite plants. Lazy as they are, they will eat the bait that is closest to them, and become stunned. Putting the bait out in the early evening and collecting the paralyzed slugs in the early morning is generally the best tactic. Autumn is the best time to bait, as the slugs and snails are getting ready to lay their eggs in the moist ground that comes with the fall rains.

Do be aware that pets, birds and other small animals may also be drawn to the attractant in the bait. For this reason, it is best to use the traps where you can place the bait safely out of the reach of pets (or even children) but still be accessible to the slugs and snails. There are several traps available commercially or you can make one by cutting small holes near the top of an empty cottage cheese container, put some bait in it, replace the lid and sink it slightly into the ground or put a rock on top to keep it from tipping over. By not sinking it so the holes are level with the ground, the slugs can still crawl in but the ground beetles will not. And ground beetles are some of the good guys that prey on slugs and snails.

Other slug and snail predators include toads, frogs, snakes, and birds, so it helps to encourage these creatures in your garden.

A less toxic chemical to use as bait is iron phosphate. But it is also less effective to the slugs and snails. Changing the place you bait and what you use is helpful, as the slugs will learn after about two weeks where not to eat and what not to eat. For a creature with no brain, they are surprisingly smart. Using the flaky or pellet forms of metaldehyde bait is not recommended around birdfeeders, as some of it looks like seed and the birds will eat it and be poisoned. Use a liquid form here. The flakes are great under groundcovers or in traps, though.

Beer. An old wives' tale? No, not really. The slugs and snails are attracted to the yeast in the beer and will dive in. For some reason not known to me, slugs will die in about 30 minutes if left in beer. They do not seem to drown, but are poisoned by the beer's alcohol. When held under plain water, however, they will take up to 12 hours to die. A mixture of one-half teaspoon brewers yeast, one teaspoon sugar, two teaspoons flour and two cups of water makes a good bait and is nontoxic to pets.

So now that you have collected all these paralyzed slugs and snails, what do you do with them? Throwing them across the road to be hit by traffic is random at best, and they will only crawl back, as they are territorial. It won't help to place them in the brush pile or the compost pile as they will crawl from those places as well. Cutting them in half with pruners works, as they do not regenerate from separate parts, but it is a gruesome thing to do. So my recommendation—and the easiest—is to place them in a sealed trash bag and throw them out.

An extra tip: getting the slime off your hands can be tricky as it absorbs water. "Wash" your hands with dirt or vinegar to remove the slime instead. Better yet, wear gloves when collecting slugs or snails. And remember, we can only hope to control slugs and snails; we have no chance of eliminating them.

Box Elder Bugs (Leptocoris rubrolineatus)

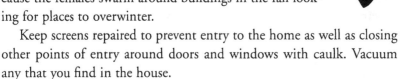

An elongated oval bug about a half inch in length, the western box elder bug is dull black or dark brown with narrow orange-red markings along each side and outlining its wings. A true bug, the wings cross over its back. It does little damage to trees and shrubs, but it will cause blemishes in fruit. Mostly, they are considered annoying because the females swarm around buildings in the fall looking for places to overwinter.

Keep screens repaired to prevent entry to the home as well as closing other points of entry around doors and windows with caulk. Vacuum any that you find in the house.

Root Weevils (Otiorhynchus sulcatus)

Root weevils are more of a problem at the larvae stage when they feed on the roots of ornamental shrubs such as rhododendrons. In a serious infestation, the weevil larvae can weaken the shrub, causing wilting or even die-back. Adult root weevils feed at night on foliage, and the notched edges where they have eaten the leaves are the first indicators of a problem. The adults also feed on lilac, euonymus, and clematis. Weevils winter in the larval stage at the host plants' roots. Adults emerge in the early spring or late summer and feed for three to four weeks before laying eggs. The eggs are laid during the summer and hatch soon after, beginning to feed on the roots as larvae. By fall they are nearly full grown and will remain in a nonfeeding stage as long as the ground around the plant remains cool. There is one generation per year.

Begin monitoring in June for the adults. When you first see the signs of notching on the leaves, it is time to find out how serious a problem you have. Going out at night with a piece of white paper and shaking the branch will generally dislodge the adults and they will fall onto the paper. Timing for chemical control is important. Drenching the soil in the fall to kill larvae is most effective. Foliar applications will only affect the adults and so should be applied during the months when they are feeding. Sticky traps placed around the trunk of the shrub can also be effective in catching the adults as they climb the trunk to feed.

Leafcutter Bees (Megachile fidelis)

This little bee is less than a half inch long but is marked like most bees in black with yellow stripes. Its damage will most likely be seen as notched foliage on roses or ash trees. The females are solitary and each raises its own young. They rapidly cut circular notches in the leaves and remove the fragments to line the nests that are made in rotting wood or in the soil. They will lay one egg in each cell after having stocked it with pollen and nectar, food for the larvae.

Most leafcutter bees have a coastal range from California to Oregon. Unless you are infested with a large colony, leafcutter bee damage will be minimal. The best control when a serious problem occurs is to cover the roses with a fine netting. Please keep in mind that most leafcutter bees are native species and act as good pollinators of native plants. Chemical control, therefore, should be used as a last resort, and only for very serious infestations.

Leafminers

Leafminer is a general term that encompasses a wide variety of insects that burrow between the layers of a leaf. Most are named for the host plant, such as the spinach leafminer, the lilac leafminer, and the columbine leafminer. Mostly the symptoms are meandering pale green lines through the leaves. Some are more blotchy than others and the tentiform leafminers construct little tentlike structures that arise from the leaf. When they are finished feeding, they emerge from the leaf and drop to the ground to pupate. They can create about two or three generations each year.

Leafminers rarely cause a serious problem and the best control is to pluck off the first leaf you see infected. Chemicals are ineffective as the miners are protected by the leaf structure once they enter it. But there are lots of natural enemies for leafminers and the plants will usually be able to outgrow the damage, so the best tactic is to leave them alone and they will generally disappear.

European Cranefly (Tipula paludosa)

We first panic when we see a European cranefly as we think it is a gigantic mosquito. The adult of this species actually does very little harm. It is the larvae that are problematic. With a voracious appetite, the larvae infest our lawns and can cause them to thin in the spring when they should be vigorously growing. The larvae are about one and a half inches long and look like a gray or brown worm with a leathery skin. They hatch in late summer and feed through the entire winter on the roots, crowns, and shoots of the turf. The damage will be evident any time between January and May. Starlings and other birds may be active on the lawn, which can create more damage as they dig for the larvae. Moles will also be evident as they feed on the larvae as well.

Generally, digging a six-square-inch area from the turf and inspecting it will clue you in if you have a problem. Six larvae or more in that six-inch square, or if turf damage is evident, will indicate a problem worth dealing with.

Cranefly larvae are easily controlled with insecticides. Begin monitoring for problems in January, and check with your extension agent to verify the insecticides that are permitted for homeowners' use in your area.

Sawfly

Sawfly is another case where the adult is less of a problem than the larvae. The western willow (*Cimbex pacifica*) adult sawflies are about an inch long and are found from coastal California to Washington. The rusty willow sawfly (*Cimbex rubida*) is found generally in coastal California. They both can be a problem when damaging large areas of the barks of willow and fruit trees (both ornamental and orchard), but the larvae skeletonize the leaves and weaken the plants considerably. Some currants, pears, cherries, and plums are affected by the pear sawfly (*Calirosa cerasi*). Pear sawflies have tiny, slimy, greenish-brown larvae that resemble small slugs. Check with your local extension office for spraying suggestions in cases of severe problems.

Coastal Gardening in the Pacific Northwest

Aphids (Aphididae)

The very large family of aphids are one of the most interesting—and prolific—of the insects that plague the northwest coast. To make a long, complicated story short, the pregnant females give birth to other pregnant females, who then can give birth in about six or seven days. As you can imagine, this allows their numbers to multiply dramatically in a single season. The adults can be born winged or wingless, depending on the availability of food. During periods of high infestation, winged aphids are born so they can seek nourishment elsewhere. They are generally pear shaped, tiny (about an eighth of an inch or less) and can be any color from clear white to pink, green, red, or brown. They suck the juices from the leaves, stems, and flowers. Most aphids are host-specific, which means they prefer one type of plant over all others. Knowing your plant will help to identify the aphid. There are rose aphids, potato aphids, lettuce aphids, tulip bulb aphids, rosy apple aphids, and many more. Aphids can produce a saliva that may be toxic to some plants and cause distortion of the newly forming leaves or flower buds. They also secrete a sweet sticky substance fondly called "honeydew" that attracts some ants. In fact, the ants are so enamored of this juice they will actually farm the aphids and milk them for the honeydew.

Fortunately there are a lot of aphid enemies, including ladybug beetles, syrphid flies, and parasitic wasps. If these beneficial insects aren't doing their job fast enough to suit you, a strong spray of water will generally dislodge and kill the aphids. For a mild rose aphid infestation, gently rubbing them off the buds with your fingers can also help with the problem. Pruning prior to the rose buds breaking in the very early spring will remove the eggs that may have wintered over in the rose canes. No worries, the buds will regrow.

As far as chemical controls go, many of the systemic rose foods will include something to control aphids as well as the fungal diseases. For other plants, horticultural oils and insecticidal soaps are also effective but need to be reapplied on a frequent basis, including the underside of the leaves.

Thrips (Thysanoptera)

Thrips are such tiny, slender insects that they appear to be nothing more than black dots moving over a plant, most being about 1/32 of an inch or smaller. There are over 600 species in North America alone. You can determine if you have thrips by breathing heavily on the "black dots." Because they react to the carbon dioxide in your breath, thrips will move when they come in contact with it. The majority of thrips have fringed wings, but they are so small they need magnification to be seen. And many species of thrips have no wings at all.

Thrips generally overwinter in the adult stage in most of the Pacific Northwest. The adults seek out flowers for feeding as well as laying eggs. Injuries are generally minor but a severe infestation will blemish the flowers or distort the petals. Flower thrips, onion thrips, and gladiolus thrips are generally host specific. Except that now scientists are finding that flower thrips can be a major vector for tomato spotted wilt. This includes the infestations that affects peppers as well. Gladiolus thrips can be very damaging when the insect punctures the tissues and sucks the plant's sap. Infested leaves will appear silvery to begin with and later turn brown and die. A heavy infestation can possibly prevent flowering. These thrips can also damage the gladiolus corms in storage. If you find the corms have become sticky or dark from plant sap at the wounds, they need to be disinfected. Do this by dropping them into a very hot water bath (112–120 degrees F.) for about 20 to 30 minutes. Gladiolus thrips will also feed on irises and lilies, but these plants are less damaged than the gladiolus.

Adult thrips seem to prefer dark or blue flowers. Overhead irrigation will kill many thrips as will heavy rains. So it seems odd that thrips can be a problem on the coast. Perhaps because some species are migratory, they are problematic in selected areas only.

Chemical control has generally proven to be ineffective except in greenhouse situations.

Caterpillars and Cutworms

Caterpillars that kill seedling plants are often described as cutworms. Caterpillars are nothing more than the larvae stages of butterflies and moths. Cutworms can be damaging to vegetable crops and ornamental shrubs, and are generally host specific. Some caterpillars are beneficial, like that of the harvester butterfly (*Feniseca tarquinius*) that devours aphids. Before you spray for caterpillar damage, be certain to identify the caterpillar as well as its adult form. I know a woman who routinely sprayed to eliminate all her caterpillars and wondered why she had no butterflies in her garden. A good butterfly/moth/caterpillar guide book is valuable here.

Cutworms are named as such because they tend to cut and kill the seedlings. Other types of cutworms such as the yellow striped army-worm (*Spodoptera ornithogalli*) are able to crawl all over the plant and feast on leaves and flowers as well as the young plants. Most cutworms produce one generation per season. Most also lay their eggs among weeds or vegetation during the late summer. Other cutworms' moths cannot survive even the mildest of our winters and migrate to the southern coastal areas, so their damage is more sporadic than the ones with the ability to overwinter. The term "miller" most often applies to the moth (adult) stage of the army cutworms (*Euxoa auxiliaris*).

Ground beetles, toads, snakes, and spiders are the best predators of army cutworms. Parasitic wasps are also helpful in control. Weed control can be effective to avoid the laying of eggs in dense vegetation in late summer. Tilling the garden in the fall and spring will also eliminate many cutworms, as will using transplants in the garden rather than young seedlings. Protect the transplants with a barrier such as clean milk jugs or plastic cups. Light in the evening should be avoided in the vegetable garden as it will attract the adult moths.

Chemical baits appear to be more effective than sprays or dusts as they can be more selectively spread around the base of infected plants.

Cucumber Beetles

Two different cucumber beetles affect northwest vegetable gardens. The striped cucumber beetle (*Diabrotica acalymma vittata*) is a small, green beetle that has three black stripes down its back. Its larvae is active when the soil reaches at least 53 degrees. The western spotted cucumber beetle (*Diabrotica undecimpunctata*) is more of a yellow-green and has black spots on its back. Both usually do the most damage when cucumber plants are young, enjoying the emerging seedlings. Because of the timing of this, they may retard the plants' development or even kill them. They will later gather in large groups in the flowers of squash and chew the pits of fruits. Larvae of these beetles feed on the plants' roots, doing little damage there, but they will move to the rind of developing cucumbers. The adults can also transmit bacteria that will cause cucumber mosaic virus.

Row covers are helpful early in the season but should be removed when the plants begin to flower so they can be pollinated. Limit watering when the fruits ripen to avoid the larvae tunneling through moist soil to feed on the fruit. Mulches can also be helpful to combat the larval tunneling.

Chemical controls may be helpful. Check with your extension agent to see which ones are registered for homeowner use in your state.

Lace Bug (Stephanitis rhododendri)

Also known as rhododendron lace bug, this is a small, flat, gray bug about a quarter inch or less in size. They have lacy patterns on their heads, thorax, and front wings. They can be very harmful to ornamental

shrubs, especially rhododendrons, because in the fall, the females lay their eggs in slits they cut on the underside of
leaves. The plant then secretes sap to heal itself and this
dries to form a small projection from the leaf that protects
the eggs over the winter. Eggs hatch in mid to late spring.
The several varieties of lace bugs suck the sap from the leaves of trees
and shrubs, which can eventually cause the death of plant tissue and
significant damage to the plant.

Several chemical controls will help when applied in late spring when
the nymphs appear from the hatched eggs. Keep in mind, most chemicals will require multiple applications to be effective.

Mosquitoes (Culicidae)

We who live near the ocean shore are spoiled
with the lack of substantial mosquito populations.
But don't be fooled into thinking they are not a
coastal problem. Take three steps into any of the
coastal mountain ranges in midsummer, and you
will be attacked by this efficient predator.

Males have very feathery antennae, which the
females do not possess. But the females are the ones who require a
blood meal before they can lay eggs. Mosquitoes are more of a *gardener's*
problem than a garden problem as they do not harm the plants. More
than their annoying bites, they can be vectors for serious diseases of humans, birds, and animals. Prevention is the best cure. Eliminate sources
of standing water, for example in ponds or containers, or even old tires,
to keep eggs from hatching. In a pond or other garden feature with
standing water, have a few goldfish that will feed on mosquito larvae.
By reducing their breeding areas, we can better control their populations.

Because mosquito control is best done over large areas, community
governments often organize the pesticide applications when a severe
problem has been identified. There is a good source of information for
the northwest at the Northwest Mosquito and Vector Control Association. This nonprofit organization helps communities through the region
by providing control information. They can be reached at www.nwmvca
.org or by mailing to NWMVCA, 521 First Avenue NW, Great Falls,
MT 59404.

Flea Beetles (Coleoptera)

Another expansive family of beetles are the flea beetles, a tiny member (about one-quarter inch) of the beetle family. There are flea beetles

named for potatoes, eggplants, tubers, cabbage, and tobacco, and most of them are blue-black or brown, are capable of jumping from leaf to leaf, and chew circular holes on the leaves of other plants as well as their namesakes. The cabbage flea beetles, for example, also feast on lettuces and beets. Strong fliers, the cabbage flea beetles can infest wide garden areas. The adults chew pits into the leaves and the females choose the areas around the base of the plants to lay their eggs. The larvae are very small and do little damage to the plants' root hairs on which they feed. They do pupate in the root area, though, and emerge as adult beetles. Generally there are about three generations per season at about 45- to 50-day intervals.

Most of the flea beetles spend the winter in the adult stage under any type of protective debris. The "potato/tomato" flea beetles, which affect the nightshade plants such as tomatoes, potatoes, and eggplants, become more active as the temperatures warm above 50 degrees in the spring. The tuber flea beetle larvae does more damage to the potato tubers than do the other types of beetle larvae. This species of beetle generally has only one generation per year and will move to seek winter shelter by midsummer. There are no chemicals that are registered for use by homeowners to control tuber flea beetles.

Fortunately, most healthy plants can outgrow damage from flea beetles. Floating row covers can be effective to protect seedlings. Using larger transplants can also help with control. The cabbage flea beetle will need to be controlled during the establishment of heads for broccoli, cabbage, and cauliflower. Sowing radishes around the broccoli has shown some promise in repelling the cabbage flea beetles.

Seedlings of tomatoes and eggplant will no doubt need some extra protection during their development as well. Row covers will also work against the potato/tomato flea beetles. Some chemical controls are available for severe infestations but are more likely to be required in a commercially producing field in late May. Chinese cabbage and mustards will need more serious control, too.

Whiteflies (Trialeurodes vaporariorum)

Whiteflies are mostly a problem in greenhouses on the coast. In fact, they have been called "greenhouse whiteflies." As nymphs and adults, they feed on greenhouse plants of almost any type and weaken them by sucking the sap from the plants. While feeding, they excrete a "honeydew" sticky substance that will contaminate the fruits, flowers, and vegetables. Because they came originally from subtropical and tropical areas, they cannot survive even a mild coastal winter outdoors, and so seek shelter in homes and greenhouses.

Whiteflies are difficult to control once established in a greenhouse or home, so the best tactic is to not introduce them. Inspect all plants you are bringing into a greenhouse and if necessary, quarantine them in a different location for about two weeks before installing them into the greenhouse. Nymphs do not move after settling in to feed, and they will be killed if their host plant dies. Adult whiteflies will also die after a few days if their food source is removed.

Yellow sticky tape traps can be effective in catching adult whiteflies. They are also repelled by light-colored mulches. Insecticidal soaps can be effective with repeat applications on both sides of the leaves. Other chemicals are less effective, and many are not cleared for use on edible crops.

Beneficial Insects

Before leaving the subject of insects, let me say a few words about the beneficials. These include bees, butterflies, parasitic wasps, lacewings, soldier beetles, dragonflies, preying mantises, and spiders (which are not insects, but arachnids—we just tend to think of them as insects).

Bees are considered beneficial to us because they are the Great Pollinators. However, many areas of North America have been noticing a dramatic drop in the number of honeybees since the mid-1990s. This has been the case in the Pacific Northwest as well. While insecticides were thought to be the primary culprit, it has since been found that two types of introduced mites have had more of a detrimental effect than some of the agricultural pesticides. Beekeepers are finding ways to deal with this decline and many feel the native bees will step up to fill the void. But most of the native bees do not form colonies and prefer to live as solitary bees. An important introduction has been the mason bees. These bees will colonize if provided proper housing. Simple boards drilled with several rows of two-inch-deep holes and hung in a sheltered location may entice mason bees to your yard.

Parasitic wasps, ladybug beetles, soldier beetles, lacewings, and preying mantises are examples of insects that feed on the insects we find to be damaging in our gardens. Remember, the presence of beneficial predators will only be encouraged if no pesticides are used in the garden. The numbers of predators will fluctuate accord-ing to the amount of food available as well. Large quantities of ladybugs will only be seen if there are large quantities of aphids. When one population declines, the other will rise, and vice versa, equaling out the numbers of each.

Butterflies, damselflies, and dragonflies are considered beneficial insects primarily because they are pretty. But they are not just a pretty face and are valuable to have in the garden. Damselflies are thinner than dragonflies and all of their wings have a similar shape. Dragonflies are thicker in their bodies and their back wings are broader than the front. But both cruise plants looking for insects, which they can pluck off leaves while in flight.

While spiders are less welcome in the garden, it's generally because they have a bad reputation. Only two spiders in the Pacific Northwest are known to be poisonous: the aggressive house spider, also known as the hobo spider, and the black widow spider. The black widow (*Latrodectus mactans*) prefers the drier areas of the northwest, however, and is rarely seen on the coast. It is a shiny black spider and has a red hourglass shape on its stomach. They are quite shy and will run from most human contact, only biting when threatened. The female does kill the males after mating, but this is common among a lot of spider species. Her web is usually very disjointed and not at all the neatly woven web of the yellow garden spider (*Argiope aurantia*).

Aggressive house spiders (*Tegenaria agrestis*) are a reddish brown in color and have an inverted V or chevron patterns on their back. They also have ringed markings on their legs, with short leg hairs. Male hobo spiders are more common than females, and their venom is more poisonous as well, making them more of a threat.

Other than these two, spiders should be welcome in the garden. You will see more spiders in the fall, as that is when they mate. For more control of spiders, use yellow bulbs in outdoor lights, as spiders tend to build their webs near white light. Wear gloves when handling wood or storage boxes. Sweep the webs from the corners of the house, closets, and windows, as well as outside from trees and shrubs, gates, and arbors. Try not to kill them when you find them indoors, but use a piece of paper instead to remove them gently to an outdoor location.

CRITTERS

When you are diagnosing plant problems, you may find that neither diseases nor insects are involved. It may be a four-legged creature that is creating the most visible damage to your gardens.

There are two schools of thought concerning "invaders." The first is that your garden should be pristine and not be subject to the munching and tunneling of anyone but you and your family. The opposing view is that the animals were here first and should be tolerated if not actually encouraged.

Both ways of looking at gardening have their inherent troubles. The first opinion will be difficult to hold because you will get to feel like

The Enforcer. What animals will you tolerate and what ones will be prohibited entry? Will your yard become The Forbidden Garden, where only the invited may visit? It could get to be a full-time job to patrol a reasonably sized garden. Or will you install a very high electric fence to control entry? Ah, but what about the moles, chipmunks, and squirrels that tunnel under or climb over that giant fence?

After all, the creatures of the woods were the first residents of the coast. Deer and elk, squirrels and chipmunks were here long before *Homo erectus* arrived or that first ship landed or the first pioneers felled trees to homestead. The native mammals and birds learned to fend for themselves using the native plants that were here; plants that would re-grow without being pampered. It was only when we humans brought rose bushes and tasty ornamental plants that these creatures discovered the smorgasbord that is our garden and learned to love the idea that we supply their food for them so they no longer need to forage for it.

But, then again, do we really want to see our hard work and consid-erable investment walk away in the stomach of Bambi? Elk are even worse, as they browse in large herds and can completely wipe out a gar-den in a few hours if they like what is on the menu. If we could train the elk and the deer to prune our plants properly, maybe we wouldn't be so reluctant to have them in the yard. Perhaps by knowing our enemies, we can better learn how to, if not control them, at least live in harmony with them. We need to find a balance.

Chewed bark on cambium tissue of small trees will most likely indi-cate the presence of small mammals such as mice or squirrels. Teeth marks will generally be evident.

We must have a "no-tolerance policy" against rats and mice, both of which can carry disease and become very destructive to buildings as well as gardens. Both types of rodents are nocturnal, so we often are not aware of their presence until a large colony has become established.

Larger trees and shrubs will show evidence of larger animals like elk and deer or even escaped horses or cattle by the torn branches and cut-off flower tops. Deer and elk love tender new shoots of everything from lilies and lobelia to roses. Even the thorny branches don't seem to deter them. However, most will avoid herbs. Plant lavender and rosemary, echinacea and agastache to discourage deer from feeding in your garden. They are also said to dislike ornamental grasses, although that isn't the case with an elk herd, as they are less discriminating in their tastes.

Rats and Mice

Both Norway and roof rats are found along the coastal areas, espe-cially in towns with shipping interests. Norway rats (*Rattus norvegicus*) are large, about 15 inches long in total length and can be colored gray, brown, or nearly black. Roof rats (*Rattus rattus*) are as long as their Norwegian cousins but generally less sturdy in build. Their tails are longer than their bodies and the stomach is often white.

Common house mice (*Mus musculus*) are almost as destructive as rats and are often confused with young rats. But the mice have proportionately smaller heads and feet.

Both kinds of rodents generally move along regular paths and have defined runs. Rats can leave trails through the gardens and dig or eat two- to three-inch holes around the foundations of buildings.

To control these undesirable visitors, there are four important steps that must be followed. The first is to eliminate their shelter. Block spaces under buildings. Reduce any shrubbery or vegetation around the foundation of buildings and raise woodpiles or stacks of building materials, where rats like to nest, at least eight inches off the ground. Higher than that is even better but may not be practical. Block any old burrows you can find.

The second step is to make all of your structures rodent-proof, including any garages, potting sheds, and greenhouses, as well as your home. Barns and older, larger structures are more difficult to rodent-proof, but even a small effort will help. Close any openings larger than one-third inch in diameter that they can get their teeth into to enlarge. Seal openings around drains and pipes. Cover the bottom edges of doors with heavy metal or wire mesh. Use rat guards on pipes, wires, or anywhere else they may climb.

Elimination of their food and water is step three and is, in fact, crucial in rodent control. Store any human and pet food in rodent-proof containers. Use tightly covered metal garbage cans for waste disposal. Clean up any pet droppings, as rats will be able to survive nicely on feces. Do not give outside pets any more food than they can eat at one sitting. Be aware that any birdseed scattered on the ground will be irresistible to rodents, including squirrels, as it is an easy meal.

The final step is to kill any existing rodents. You may prefer poisons over using a trap. There are a wide variety of rodenticides on the market, all of which serve a different purpose and location. As always, read the labels before you purchase a product and before each time you use it. Protect yourself by wearing gloves and protect your children and pets by placing the poisons out of their reach. Use a variety of products, as rats can become tolerant of poisons. Talk to your local extension agent or wildlife control agent with any questions. And don't underestimate the use of a good cat.

Gophers (Thomomys *species*)

While pocket gophers are most prevalent east of the Cascade Mountain Range, some are working their way west toward the coast. Burrowing rodents, they create mounds that are fan-shaped, with all the dirt thrown in one direction. There is usually an open hole on one side of the mound. They feed almost entirely on plant matter that they find below the ground, and so can be very destructive in a garden. They are about five inches long with a two- or three-inch tail. They are usually brown or gray and have visible buck teeth. The females can breed one to three times each year, depending on the availability of food. Control is most effective when new mounds appear in the spring and fall. Traps and poisonous baits are effective. Traps must be placed back to back in the main run, which is found by probing about 12 inches away from the mound. If a catch isn't made in a few days, relocate the trap.

Toxic baits also need to be placed in the main run. Bait each tunnel system in several places for best results.

Moles

Moles are often blamed for the damage done by gophers, but most of the time moles are only interested in the insects underground. There are four separate species in the northwest but the one most problematic for coastal gardens is the coast mole (*Scapanus orarius*). While they will not eat plant matter, they create tunnels that are very destructive to lawns and gardens. Mole mounds differ from gophers in that they are round, without an evident opening. Their diet consists mainly of earthworms, grubs, and insects. By eliminating grubs in the lawn areas, the moles will usually move elsewhere. They may sample a nibble or two of a root crop or seeds, but are not usually the problems of these plants that gophers can be.

Active all year, moles mate in the early spring and have a litter of three or so from March to May. The only guaranteed way of controlling a real mole problem is by trapping. There are several types of mole traps available, but they must be placed according to the directions for best results. And again, you must find an active tunnel to place the trap. Stomp down molehills in the afternoon and by morning you will be able to tell which tunnels are active because they will have been rebuilt. During much of the year no activity will be obvious.

Most mole baits are ineffective and can be expensive. Fumigants or mothballs and chewing gum have not been proven to be effective except as old wives tales. Again, try a cat. My cat, Gertrude (named after Miss Jekyll, of course) routinely brings moles and voles as gifts to my husband and me.

*Voles (*Microtus *species)*

Most of the damage to plants accredited to moles is actually done by voles using the moles' tunnels. Voles are smaller and are plant eaters. They are small and short-eared and can do considerable damage to tree roots and will girdle trunks. They love the plants in a vegetable garden and feast on the root crops, bulbs, and tubers. They are active all day and night and in all seasons. They are also supporters of large families having as many as 5 litters a year with up to 11 young in each litter.

Looking for gnawed roots and root crops with small grooves that are front teeth marks will help identify a vole problem. Management of the vegetation is the key in vole control. Mow the grass between rows in an orchard and keep it short. Thatch the lawn to prevent hiding places. Do not mulch up to the trunk of a tree or shrub. The voles love a loose mulch with a tasty tree to gnaw on. Pick up fallen fruits so voles will not have them to eat. Keep garden areas free of weeds, excess vegetation, and tall grass, and harvest root vegetables before winter. The use of regular mousetraps baited with peanut butter or apple can sometimes help with small populations. Dig into the tunnels to place the trap and cover with a board for easy access and removal. Check the traps daily. No chemical baits are registered for homeowner use on voles at the present time in Oregon and Washington. Check with your extension agents if you live elsewhere.

Deer and Elk

Blacktail deer (*Odocoileus hemionis columbianus*) can be real problems for certain types of gardens along the coast, especially ones in mountainous areas. Roosevelt elk (*Cervus elephus roosevelti*) are also found in the coastal areas in the winter and in the coastal mountains during the summers. They generally do not come to the dunes, although I know many gardeners who would dispute this. The best control is a tall fence. But make it an obvious, visible fence so the animals won't accidentally stampede into it.

Plastic, fine mesh cloths can sometimes be draped over individual plants or areas as a deterrent, and these generally blend in with the plants' foliage. But this mesh must be lifted as the plants grow or the deer and elk will simple eat the new shoots as they grow through the mesh. In the case of large herds of elk, substantial wire cages may need to be constructed to protect the shrubs.

Planting deer-resistant plants is also an option. However, deer may take a liking to something in your yard that they will leave alone in a neighbor's, and both deer and elk will eat almost anything if hungry enough. Deer generally avoid herbs and ornamental grasses as mentioned before. Friends tell me their large, barking dogs help to deter deer as well, but no formal research that I can find has been done on that suggestion.

Mountain Beavers *(Aplodontia rufa)*

These cute little guys are said to be among the world's most primitive living rodent. They actually are not beavers at all but are more closely related to squirrels. And they don't live in the high mountains, either. Also known as chehalis, boomers, whistlers, or sewellels, they look like muskrats without tails and generally weigh about two to four pounds and are about a foot long. Their large digging claws allow them to dig shallow but large tunnels for access to their main food sources of sword ferns, blackberries, and salals. But their territories can range up to a half an acre and they will eat almost any kind of vegetation when hungry, including onion family members like allium and chives, sometimes stashing it outside their burrow entrances.

Mountain beavers usually destroy more vegetation than they eat, which is even more annoying to most gardeners. They especially like rhododendrons and will clip off lower branches, leaving only the stub. They will also chew the bark from the base of large trees.

If a single tree is affected, a wire cage around the base may be sufficient to discourage mountain beaver activity. In the case of more destruction, you may resort to trapping and relocating the animal. Repellants have not proven to be effective, and no poisons are recommended. If you are trapping them, do so in mild weather as they are prone to hypothermia and shouldn't be left in the traps for long periods of time. Check the traps daily, baiting them with a large piece of apple or sweet potato. Cover the trap with a tarp and place the trap at the entrance to its burrow. The tarp will guide the animal from the burrow into the trap and protect it from the elements until you can relocate him.

Raccoons *(Procyon lotor)*

Few of us would fail to recognize the masked "bandit" we call a raccoon. Native to much of the United States and Canada, this mammal can weigh as much as 50 pounds and has very successfully adapted to human society. Virtually fearless, this is a large animal that is seen not only in the wild but has moved into the suburbs and even into major cities to forage for food. At the coast, they are less of a problem because their main diet is the abundant seafood found here. But they are good climbers and with such force behind their considerable weight, they can easily tip over loaded garbage cans during their late-night forays into civilization. They can also invade unattended houses and leave quite a mess behind. In some areas they are carriers of rabies and so should be excluded from neighborhoods where possible.

Control of raccoons is primarily limited to trapping them and removing them from the area. But this must be approved by local wildlife or animal control departments. Best to remove food sources by locking away the trash cans and blocking any possible entries into buildings. The presence of a loud dog is sometimes a deterrent. The biggest problem with raccoons in your coastal garden will most likely be the raiding of pond fish in the night. A net on the surface of the pond water and good places for the fish to hide will most likely discourage future forays.

Squirrels

The only coastal ground squirrel in Oregon and California is the California ground squirrel (*Spermophilus*). They feed mostly on vegetation and can easily damage a garden. They are generally dormant during the winter and the hottest parts of the summer. Certain species can reach population densities of over 100 per acre, as they breed in single litters of 2 to 10 young in the spring.

Exclude them from buildings using the same methods as for rats and mice. Fencing doesn't work for obvious reasons, nor do scare tactics. Generally ground squirrels are not protected, but check with local authorities before using lethal methods. Trapping can be effective, but it may not be legal to release them back into the wild. Lethal traps used for rats may work, as do fumigants placed into the burrows. Poisons and baits are not registered for use on this type of rodent.

Tree squirrels are found throughout the Pacific Northwest and the most frequent coastal visitor is the native Douglas squirrel (*Tamiasciurus douglasi*). Unmistakable with it dark red coats and orange stomach, this squirrel is common west of the Cascade Range. Another native squirrel now being seen along the coast is a gray squirrel (*Sciurus griseus*). This squirrel is shy but large.

Squirrels generally become pests when they attack fruit, nut, and vegetable crops. They also raid bird feeders and can damage ornamental trees and shrubs by stripping the bark. Native squirrels are protected by law so they must be cage-trapped and released, repelled, or excluded rather than lethally dealt with. Nonnative species are better euthanized rather than spreading these invasive, destructive animals into a new area. Eliminate food sources, especially around bird feeders. Clean up fallen fruits and nuts and use squirrel-proof bird feeders. Make sure the attic vents are covered and protect bulbs with heavy plastic mesh cages when planting. Metal guards can be placed around tree trunks but this method is not effective if other, taller trees are present for the squirrels to use as "launching pads."

TOLERANCE

It is important to determine your level of tolerance for all these pests. Slight insect damage and squirrels at the bird feeders may be acceptable to you. Diseases will be less acceptable because of their propensity to spread and infect more plants.

Encouraging natural predators will help with pest and insect control. Proper sanitation of the ground around the plants and correct planting to allow good air circulation will help with disease control. While chemicals are sometimes necessary with severe problems, they are generally not the only solutions. Chemical controls should only be used as a last resort after all other methods have been tried and failed. This is what is known as Integrated Pest Management. It will keep your garden healthier in the long run. Limited use of chemicals is especially important, living as close as we do to oceanic and riparian areas. What we do in our gardens will have an ultimate effect on wildlife and our water tables. Even overfertilization can have adverse affects on our water.

By being responsible gardeners, we can protect our gardens, our wildlife, and our environment.

SEVEN

PLANTS TO AVOID IN
COASTAL GARDENS

I T IS EASY TO PUT TOGETHER a list of plants that will do well along the coast, and I have included examples in the previous chapters. It is more difficult to give suggestions of plants not to bother trying. Time, experience, and visits with other gardeners have given me ideas of things I don't want to bother with, and I will share a few here, along with the reasons I have eliminated them from my plant choices. Keep in mind that some dedicated gardeners will have no problems with some of the plants I am listing. But I have included them in the interest of a readily sustainable garden.

The first is the peony. Peonies are beautiful and I find some coastal gardeners do have success with them. I personally find them impossible because they like full sun, no wind—especially no salt-laden wind. So I don't even bother. Instead I visit my friends' peonies when I go inland.

Another plant that is difficult—but not impossible—are the hybrid tea roses. We have already discussed roses at length in chapter 4 on cottage gardens. And there are many coastal gardeners who have great success with hybrid teas. This is due mostly to the time, energy, and cost they are willing to put into growing these beautiful but temperamental roses. Hybrid teas are susceptible to black spot, powdery mildew, and other fungal diseases that can be prevalent in coastal areas where winter rains are the norm. If you have the interest and the time, certainly put in a rose or two to try. Give them a spot in full sun, protected from strong winds and you will have a better chance of success. There are several hybrid tea roses that are disease resistant that may work for you. Notice I said "disease resistant" not "disease immune." To my knowledge, there is no rose yet that is completely resistant to the fungal diseases. This may change in a few years. As it stands now, several roses bred today have less tendency to be affected by black spot, but it can still be an issue. If you must have a rose, try 'Simplicity' or 'Climbing Blaze'. The fewer the flower petals the better, because they will bloom easier. Many of the newer roses also lack any scent at all, being bred more for form and hardiness. *Rosa rugosa* is popular on the coast, as it is a native and will do well with less effort. They also make great hedges with thick thorns, so be cautious as to where they are placed. Near a driveway where visitors will bump into them is probably not the best location. They would be good for less used areas where you want to discourage traffic.

Photinia hedges are beautiful, and you will see many of them along the coast. But they are very prone to fungal diseases and thus it is difficult to grow a pretty, black spot–free photinia. I have two in my garden that were here when we moved in and I cut them back severely about every two years to stimulate new growth. Even so, the plants seem to attract the fungus. If my husband didn't love their red-tipped color so much, I probably would remove them altogether.

Corn, eggplant, and the large beefsteak-type tomatoes make my list of problematic plants. There aren't enough heat units each summer on the coast to ripen corn, sad to say. The same goes with the large tomatoes and eggplants. The last two are perhaps worth a try if you have a heated greenhouse. And if you must have tomatoes (and I must!) try a smaller-sized cherry or grape tomato and place it in full sun, protected from the wind. 'Honeybunch' makes a great container tomato for the patio. There are some other varieties that do well on the coast. These are listed in chapter 5's special section on tomatoes.

As for trees, maples other than the Japanese maples (*Acer palmatum*) and the native vine and big-leaf maples don't seem to do well on the coast. Of course there are exceptions to this statement as well. But I find the maples prefer better defined seasonal changes than coastal gardens usually have. They like a cold winter and warmer summer, so may be all right for a mountainous coastal area. But they also don't do well in strong winds and their limbs can break easily. Better to try the shore pines, spruces or Western red cedar. If protected from winds, the Japanese maples seem to do well.

Sometimes I warn about plants because they do too well on the coast. We have already discussed the dreaded English ivy and buddleia as having been used in gardens but escaped to become problem weeds. There are four others I will add to this list.

The first are crocosmia. There are lovely yellow- ('Citronella') and red-flowered ('Lucifer') crocosmia that do not seem as aggressive as the typical orange montbretia crocosmia. The orange crocosmia have escaped cultivation and are now being seen along roadsides in large clumps that will crowd out most other plants. They have small corms that grow on top of each other in a stack. Pull off the foliage and a corm will come with it. But there can be as many as five smaller corms that will remain in the ground and sprout new top growth in a matter of weeks. If you want them to be gone from your garden, dig down and remove all the corms. If you want to have the orange crocosmia in your garden, consider planting it in pots.

The second plant I consider to have done too well in the Pacific Northwest is the yellow "flag" iris (*Iris pseudacorus*). Introduced from Europe, this plant thrives in the wetter soils along the coast and can be found from British Columbia, through Washington, and into Oregon. Pretty as it is, it is now crowding out the native iris in the wetlands. If you must have this plant, be conscientious about keeping it under control.

Number three on the hit list are the calla lilies. Personally, I love this plant with its elegant flowers and upright growth. But I know many gardeners that consider it the next thing to a weed. It will grow easily here and spreads just as easily with tiny rhizomes that you can never seem to remove. I cut mine to the ground after the flowers are done and the leaves start to brown. But even so, I find them hard to contain. Another plant best grown in pots.

The fourth thriving plant along the coast is the pampas grass (*Cortaderia selloana*). The giant plumes of this very tall, very hardy grass can be seen in gardens all along the Washington, Oregon, and Northern California coasts. It likes full sun but will grow up to twenty feet tall in any kind of soggy soil conditions or around—or in—a pond. A fast grower, this plant can reach eight feet in one season if the conditions are right. And the seeds are easily spread in the wind. Many landscapers are no longer using this plant and nurseries are loath to sell it. Yes, it is very pretty and dramatic, and if you can't part with your pampas grass, please be diligent about weeding out any new seedlings when you see them. Especially if you live near a wilderness area.

Annuals are generally pretty good on the coast because of their limited season, but there are a few that won't hold up in heavy rains. These include the annual coleus, bachelor's buttons, cockscomb, and impatiens. Since we haven't been getting heavy summer rains these last few years, these may be worth a try. Some gardeners have problems with cosmos and the Martha Washington geraniums, but they do fine for me. Marigolds are one of my slugs' favorite feasts, so I tend to plant calendula instead, as the slugs don't seem to like them as much.

Of course I won't plant English ivy or buddleia any longer and try to take out what I have. I also don't care for the chameleon plant because of its odor and its aggressive tendency. But it will do well, as will the invasive bishop's weed, vinca major, and mints. I try to stay away from all of these that I consider to be cousins to weeds. Putting them in pots or other containers may help in the case of these invasive plants.

My best advice, if you love one of the plants I have advised against, is to try them yourself and see how they do in your particular garden. You may have the dedication it takes to make them a success. And in the case of the aggressive plants, if you must have them, please keep them under control.

EIGHT

TRAVELING

ALMOST AS MUCH AS WORKING in my own gardens, I enjoy seeing other people's gardens. I wander through and marvel at what will grow in our wonderful climate. It is not practical to give locations of private gardens, so I have chosen a few public gardens that are worth visiting if you are in their area. I have found that size does not always mean quality and the smaller gardens are sometimes the best examples of what can be done in a home garden.

JAPANESE-STYLE GARDENS IN THE PACIFIC NORTHWEST

GARDEN: Nitobe Memorial Garden, University of British Columbia, Vancouver, BC, Canada
ADDRESS: 6501 Northwest Marine Drive, Vancouver, BC
HOURS: mid-March to mid-October: 10:00 a.m. to 6:00 p.m.
FEE: Yes.

Among the top five Japanese gardens outside Japan according to the "Journal of Japanese Gardens" 2004 survey. No facilities and no pets allowed. The garden was incorporated in the university campus in the late 1930s. Vandalized during World War II, it was removed in 1959 and replaced by a dormitory. Moved and reconstructed in the early 1960s, the new garden was designed by a Japanese designer to guarantee its authenticity, and it reflects the university's commitment to the Asian community. Several shades of green increase this garden's calming and reflective feel.

GARDEN: The Bloedel Reserve, Bainbridge Island, Washington
ADDRESS: 7571 Northeast Dolphin Drive, Bainbridge Island, WA
PHONE: (206) 842-7631, reservations required
HOURS: Wednesday to Sunday: 10:00 a.m. to 4:00 p.m., reservation only
FEE: Yes.

Bainbridge Island is accessible from Seattle by ferry. Call for garden reservations and allow for two hours to see them. No food services and no pets allowed. Complete with torii-style gates and an eclectic array of plant matter, this is a lovely garden to visit at any time of the year. A small gate divides the formal from the informal gardens, and a sand and rock bed was created over the old swimming pool. The Bloedels were ardent supporters of the Japanese garden at the University of Washington Arboretum and became inspired to have a Japanese garden at their estate.

GARDEN: Washington Park Arboretum Japanese Garden, Seattle, WA
ADDRESS: 1075 Lake Washington Boulevard East, Seattle, WA
HOURS: daily from 10:00 a.m., but closed Mondays, with closing times dependant on the season
FEE: Yes.

This three-acre garden was begun in 1960. The best time to visit is in the spring when the azaleas and wisteria abound. A formal pond garden is a feature here and worth strolling around in all seasons. When a fire destroyed the teahouse in the 1970s it was rebuilt and is now used for classes and for demonstrations from April through October. The garden's 10 lanterns include a three-ton one donated by Kobe, Japan, Seattle's sister city.

GARDEN: The Japanese Garden, Portland, Oregon
ADDRESS: 611 S.W. Kingston Street, Portland, OR
HOURS: October 1–March 31: Tuesday through Sunday 10:00 a.m. to 4:00 p.m., Mondays noon to 4:00 p.m.; April 1–September 30: Tuesday through Sunday 10:00 a.m. to 7:00 p.m., Mondays noon to 7:00 p.m.
FEE: Yes.

Portland's Japanese Garden came in a very close second to the Anderson Japanese Gardens in Illinois in the "Journal of Japanese Gardens" survey. This came as a surprise to many who have long considered Portland to have the best Japanese garden outside Japan. The view of Mount Hood—reminiscent of Mount Fuji—gives this garden an authentic feel. The Portland garden includes five varieties of Japanese garden styles that are seamlessly incorporated into a single garden. Impeccably maintained, this is a wonderful garden at all times of the year.

GARDEN: Mingus Park Japanese Garden, Coos Bay, Oregon
ADDRESS: 10th Avenue, Coos Bay, OR
HOURS: daylight
FEE: No.

The Mingus Park Choshi Garden honors Vietnam War casualties and was named after Coos Bay's Sister City, Choshi, Japan. The gardens were begun in 1985 and dedicated in 1996. Park across the road from the park entrance and walk along the lake to get to the Choshi Garden. Or drive up 10th Street a bit farther and park by the swimming pool and walk downhill to the garden. The garden is very traditional in its look, complete with bridges and benches placed to enjoy the view along the stream that runs through the center of the garden.

GARDEN: Shore Acres Japanese-style Garden, Coos Bay, Oregon
ADDRESS: 13080 Cape Arago Highway, Coos Bay, OR
HOURS: 8:00 a.m. to sunset
FEE: Yes.

These lovely gardens, located in Shore Acres State Park near Coos Bay, have more flowers than most traditional Japanese gardens, and are therefore more colorful but a good way to see how flowers can be incorporated into a Japanese-style garden. To arrive at the Japanese-style gardens you must first pass through formal gardens. These are also worth taking the time to stroll through. Interesting in all seasons, Shore Acres Garden is worth the trip to the ocean, about 12 miles south of Coos Bay. Re-created in the early 1990s from the original garden plans of Louis Simpson. Mr. Simpson was interested in Japanese gardens but liked to put his own spin on them, thus his choice of planting material.

GARDEN: Japanese Tea Garden at Golden Gate Park, San Francisco, California
ADDRESS: Hagiwara Tea Garden Drive; Golden Gate Park, San Francisco, CA
HOURS: 8:30 a.m. to 6:00 p.m. most days
FEE: Yes.

The Tea Gardens in San Francisco's Golden Gate Park were developed as a Japanese Village in 1894 and were converted to gardens for the California International Exposition. They are the largest and probably the oldest in California. They give a true feeling of a Japanese-style garden with teahouse, temples, and bridges as well as garden ornaments. Try to go during off-peak days and hours for the best views of the gardens themselves.

GARDEN: Japanese Friendship Garden at Kelley Park, San Jose, California

ADDRESS: Senter Road, between Phelan Avenue and Story Road, San Jose, CA

HOURS: daily, 10:00 a.m. to sunset.

FEE: Yes, for parking.

This garden was a gift to the City of San Jose by its sister city, Okayama, Japan. It is considered a fine example of a strolling garden. No pets. The cherry tree grove is a sight to behold in the spring, and gives the feeling of walking through a pink cloud. Docent-led tours are available for organizations, including a tour of the haiku stones, which have haiku inscribed on them. Situated in an Asian neighborhood in San Jose, this garden has an authentic feel, acting as a meeting place for the Asian population.

COTTAGE GARDENS IN THE PACIFIC NORTHWEST

GARDEN: Tillamook County Pioneer Museum

ADDRESS: 2106 Second Street, Tillamook, OR

FEE: Only for the museum; the gardens are free.

PARKING: Free, two-hour parking is available on all the streets surrounding the museum.

HOURS: The museum is open Tuesday through Saturday, 9:00 a.m. to 5:00 p.m.; Sundays from 11:00 a.m. to 5:00 p.m. Closed Mondays and major holidays. The gardens are accessible at all times.

HANDICAPPED ACCESSIBLE: Museum: no. Gardens: yes.

Included is an herb garden that contains plants that might have been used by the pioneers for medicinal or culinary purposes. To the east of the building is the rose garden. Many roses had been donated to the museum over the years, and during the renovation of the grounds, they were all relocated to a single area. A wooden fence surrounds the roses and protects them from the harsh winter winds. The effect is approximately fifty roses that bloom happily all summer. The rose garden is also the location of the commemorative medallion honoring the county's 150 years. Closer to the building on the east side are gardens with ornamental grasses, lilies, wildflowers, Japanese maples, and small shrubs.

To the north of the museum building are the native plants, including maidenhair ferns, manzanita, Oregon grape, and wax myrtle. A bed of Asiatic lilies stands at the northwest corner, creating a stunning display each summer.

GARDEN: The Connie Hansen Garden, Lincoln City, Oregon

ADDRESS: 1931 N.W. 33rd Street, Lincoln City, OR

HOURS: daily, 10:00 a.m. to 2:00 p.m.

FEE: Donations encouraged.

A garden at the former home of Connie Hansen, a botanist from the University of California. Mrs. Hansen began her garden in 1973 at the age of 65 and has many species of rhododendrons and azaleas as well as natives and perennials. This little acre of ground has many hundreds of plants that are protected from the coastal winds by the surrounding rhododendrons. Nice to visit at any season, but especially in the spring, when the nearly 500 rhododendrons are blooming. The Connie Hansen Garden Conservancy has owned the property since 1994 and maintains the grounds. A wonderful collection of plants that do well at the coast, as this garden is only a few blocks from the Lincoln City beaches.

GARDEN: Butterfield Cottage, Seaside Museum, Seaside, OR

ADDRESS: At the corner of Necanicum and Sixth Street, Seaside, OR From Route 101 in Seaside turn west onto First Street and then right onto Broadway, heading north of town, following signs to the Convention Center and then the museum. Turn right onto Necanicum Street after crossing the bridge over the Necanicum River. The Seaside Museum is about two blocks north on your left. Butterfield Cottage is to the south of the museum.

HOURS: Open during museum hours.

FEE: Yes, for the museum, not for the gardens.

Red currants, Japanese anemone, and *Rosa rugosa* form the outside borders of this cottage, restored by the Historical Society. Inside the garden you will find an arbor with clematis, rudbeckia and nasturtium as well as annuals and some vegetables. The garden is maintained by local garden clubs.

JOURNAL OF GARDEN VISITS

You may want to keep records of the gardens you visit here. Add photographs if you like.

Garden Name _____
Location _____
Date Visited _____
Notes _____

Garden Name _____
Location _____
Date Visited _____
Notes _____

Garden Name _____
Location _____
Date Visited _____
Notes _____

Garden Name _____
Location _____
Date Visited _____
Notes _____

Garden Name _____
Location _____
Date Visited _____
Notes _____

Garden Name _____
Location _____
Date Visited _____
Notes _____

Garden Name _____
Location _____
Date Visited _____
Notes _____

Garden Name _____

Location _____

Date Visited _____

Notes _____

Garden Name _____

Location _____

Date Visited _____

Notes _____

Garden Name _____

Location _____

Date Visited _____

Notes _____

Garden Name _____

Location _____

Date Visited _____

Notes _____

Garden Name _____

Location _____

Date Visited _____

Notes _____

Garden Name _____

Location _____

Date Visited _____

Notes _____

Garden Name _____

Location _____

Date Visited _____

Notes _____

Garden Name _____

Location _____

Date Visited _____

Notes _____

GARDENING IS A HUMBLING EXPERIENCE. A garden is never finished. Like every living thing, it evolves and changes every day. Gardening bridges the gap between the largest living things and the smallest. As gardeners, we can help to create an environment that nourishes and encourages plants and creatures to live and grow. But we also come to learn that while we may have a small say in what goes on in our gardens, there will oftentimes be forces that are beyond our control. We learn to live with nature, not control it.

We have talked a lot about the environment along the Pacific Northwest coast and how to use those climactic and oceanic conditions to our benefit as we garden. By being conscientious gardeners, we can protect the dunes, the riparian areas, and the mountains that make the Washington, Oregon, Californian, and British Columbian coasts so special. We have also discussed the beauty of the Pacific Northwest coastal areas from as far south as Monterey, California, to as far north as Vancouver Island, British Columbia. I find it inspiring that I live where people come to vacation.

No one can profess to know everything about gardening, and certainly I make no claims about being an expert gardener. I don't know any gardener who can in all honesty say they know everything there is to know. Just when we think we have learned what we need to know to create a successful garden, we realize there is so much more we can do to make it better. But I have tried to compile enough information to make you want to learn more, to try new plants or new designs, to take the time to explore your garden and experience it in a new way, to take the time not only to prune the roses but to enjoy them.

I have lived on the East Coast, in Pittsburgh, in a rural western Pennsylvania village called Ligonier, and in San Francisco. I have traveled around the world. But I must tell you that in my opinion it just doesn't get any prettier anywhere else than it is right here. Yes, we may get a lot of rain, but that's why the countryside is so green and lush. There are a lot of slugs, but they help break down the plant matter that gives our forests its nutrients. There are a few drawbacks to living near the ocean, but in my life I have never been more content than I am right here on the Oregon coast. I try every day to appreciate the beauty that surrounds me: the mountains, the birds, the ocean, the flora, and the fauna. I hope you find that contentment as well.

I HAVE FOUND THESE RESOURCES to be invaluable, not only in writing this book, but as treasured members of my personal gardening library. No coastal gardener should be without them.

Acorn, John, and Ian Sheldon. *Bugs of Washington and Oregon.* Vancouver, BC: Lone Pine Publishing, 2001.
A fun elementary book, good for children but also great drawings to help identify local insects.

Barnard, Loretta, ed. *500 Popular Shrubs and Trees for American Gardeners.* Hauppauge, NY: Barron's Educational Services, 1999.
A colorful book with good photographs and descriptions of many well-used trees and shrubs. Supplies a little information about a lot of plants.

Brenzel, Kathleen Norris, ed. *Sunset Western Garden Book.* Menlo Park, CA: Sunset Publishing Company, 2001.
The bible of many western gardeners, coastal and inland. This book has plants listed in alphabetical order and includes most everything that grows in the west. It also has great sections on suggested plants for a variety of growing conditions, including the coast.

Brown, Kendall H., and Melba Levick. *Japanese-Style Gardens of the Pacific Northwest.* New York: Rizzoli, 1999.
A lovely coffee-table book with wonderful photos as well as the histories of the major Japanese-style gardens in the northwest.

Coombes, Allen J. *Dictionary of Plant Names.* Portland, OR: Timber Press, 2002.

This book tells us the pronunciation of the botanical names. He also includes the derivations of the terms. A complement to Neal's *Gardener's Latin*, which tells what the names mean.

Cranshaw, Whitney. *Pests of the West: Prevention and Control for Today's Garden and Small Farm* (revised). Golden, CO: Fulcrum Publishing, 1998.
This book has great insight to a variety of pests and diseases that affect the coast areas as well as inland.

DeSabato-Aust, Tracy. *The Well-Tended Perennial Garden*. Portland, OR: Timber Press, 1999.
A treasured book, well thumbed and referred to because of the section on how to groom and maintain many individual perennials. Good photographs.

Fish, Margery. *Cottage Garden Flowers*. Wiltshire, UK: W.H.&L. Collingridge Limited, 1985.
First published in 1960, this little book gives further insight to the typical English cottage garden à la Gertrude Jekyll. Nice descriptions with a few black and white photographs.

Hessayon, D. G. *The Flower Expert*. London: Expert Books, 1998.
One of a series of "expert" books, this one deals strictly with flowers. Good photos and tips for care of each kind. Published in England, this book features many plants that do very well in our English-type climate of the coastal Pacific Northwest.

Houchen, Amy. *Green Afternoons, Oregon Gardens to Visit*. Corvallis, OR: Oregon State University Press, 1998.
This small book offers a compendium of public gardens to tour in Oregon, broken down into geographic areas of the state. Each garden has directions included and a brief description of what to look for in each garden. Ms. Houchen also includes three southern Washington gardens that were too close to Portland to exclude because of their interest. I have enjoyed working my way through her lists, albeit slowly.

Jekyll, Gertrude. *Colour Schemes for the Flower Garden* (reprint). Suffolk, UK: Antique Collector's Club Press, 1996.
One of my all-time favorite garden writers, this book is probably Miss Jekyll's best. Her style of writing is entertaining and much of her information holds true today. Some varieties she recommends are no longer available, but this book is worth having just for a winter's read.

Little, Elbert L. *National Audubon Society Field Guide to North American Trees (Western Region)*. New York: Alfred A. Knopf, 1980.
A good field guide for identification of trees in the West. Good photos and lots of information.

McKinley, Michael, ed. *Ortho's Home Gardener's Problem Solver*. Des Moines, IA: Meredith Books, 2001.
Although the antitheses of an organic gardener's idea of problem solving, this book offers excellent photographs useful in diagnosing plant problems. Published by chemical giant Ortho, to its credit, this book also includes nonchemical treatments for many typical garden problems.

McNeilan, Ray, and Jan McNeilan. *The Pacific Northwest Gardener's Book of Lists*. Dallas, TX: Taylor Publishing, 1997.
Lists of plants according to their needs and location. Especially helpful when looking for specific shrubs, trees, perennials, and annuals that do well on the coast.

Milne, Lorus, and Margery Milne. *National Audubon Society Field Guide to Insects and Spiders*. New York: Alfred A. Knopf, 1980.
Another good, basic field guide with loads of information about insects and spiders, with helpful photographs.

Neal, Bill. *Gardener's Latin*. Chapel Hill, NC: Algonquin Books, 1992.
A small book that defines the botanical terms used in naming plants. Some charming line drawings and bits of history are included.

Pelczar, Rita, and Peter Punzi, *American Horticultural Society: Smart Garden Regional Guide/Northwest*. New York: DK Publishing, 2003.
A relatively new series from AHS, this one divides the book into geographical locations as well as size, color, and growth habit. Good photographs.

Pettinger, April, and Brenda Costanzo. *Native Plants in the Coastal Garden*. Portland, OR: Timber Press, 2002.
A good reference guide as to how to use all those natives I have talked about.

Pojar, Jim, and Andy MacKinnon. *Plants of the Pacific Northwest Coast*. Vancouver, BC: Lone Pine Publishing, 1994.
The book I take with me in the woods but also have in an easy-to-reach location on my shelf. Good source for natives as well as plants that have invaded the northwest coastal areas.

Spellenberg, Richard. *National Audubon Society Field Guide to Wildflowers (Western Region)*. New York: Alfred A. Knopf, 2001.
Color photos and good descriptions make this the third of these Audubon guides I can't do without. The photos are grouped by flower color and shape, making it easier to find a particular plant.

Squire, David. *Cassell's Garden Directories: Cottage Gardens*. Sussex, UK: Cassell & Co., 2002.
A small book, but full of good information on how to begin a cottage garden. Lots of good photos as well as a very good plant selection guide to use as a cross reference.

Strong, Graham, and Alan Toogood. *The Mix and Match Planting Guide to Annuals and Perennials*. London: Merehurst Limited, 2000.
This fun book has color photographs that are divided on each page so you can flip back and forth to combine not only plant heights but colors and foliage. A good designing tool.

Taylor, Ronald. *Northwest Weeds: The Ugly and Beautiful Villains of Fields, Gardens and Roadsides*. Missoula, MT: Mountain Press Publishing, 1990.
A handy guide that explores weeds all over the western states.

Wiedmann, Alfred M., LaRea, J. Dennis, and Frank H. Smith. *Plants of the Oregon Coastal Dunes*. Corvallis, OR: Oregon State University Press, 1999.
This key for native plants is invaluable for identifying what is to be found on the dunes. Lots of grasses included.

Abronia latifolia, 80, **plate** 7
Abronia umbellata, 80
acanthus, 93, 107, 124
Acer circinatum, 58
Acer palmatum, 77, 125, 188, **plate** 4,
    plate 5
achillea, 103, 125
acid soil, 116
acidity of rain, 116
aconitum, 103, 125
Adiantum ferns, 121
agapanthus, 93
agastache, 93, 98, **plate** 12
Agave americana, 85
agaves, 93
aggressive house spider. *See* spider
AHS zones, 3, 4
Alchemilla mollis, 125
alder, red, 101
aloes, 93
amendment, soil, 111
American cottage gardens, 109, **plate**
    17
American River, CA, 100
Ammophila arenaria, 78
anemone, 94, 125: Japanese, **plate** 29
annual phlox, 87
annual weeds, 145
annuals, 2, 55, 56, 86, 104, 107, 109,
    112, 117, 124, 151, 152, 159, 189
anthracnose, 161
Antirrhinum majus, 124
aphids, 131, 173; controls, 173; in
    roses, 173
apple trees, 125; aphids on, 173

apron, gardening, 61
aquilegia, 121, 125
arbors, 111, 113, 179
arborvitae, American, 117
Arbutus menziesii, **122**
arches, 113
Arctotis hybrids, 107
Armeria maritima, 118
armillary spheres, 115
army cutworms, 174–75
art, in the garden, 110, 112–114
artichokes, 125, 133, 135
Aruncus dioicus, 107
ash, 161
Asian vegetables, 132
asparagus, 125
asters, 104, 125, 161; coastal wild,
    plate 15
astilbe, 107, 112, 125
Athyrium filix-femina, 121
autumn fern, **plate** 26
autumn interest, 58–59, 64
avoidance, in disease control, 158
azalea, 78, 98; deciduous
    (*Rhododendron mollis*), 64, 98, **99**;
    diseases of, 166

Baccharis pilularis, 85
bachelors buttons, 189
bacterial diseases, 71, 157, 175
bacterial slime, 158
bamboo, 144
bananas, 92, 93
bark canker, 166
basil, 131, 142

baskets, hanging, 112
baskets, mesh for bulbs, 94
bat houses, 115
beach grass, 1, 52, 78, **79**, 83, 145
beach knotweed. *See* knotweed
beans: bush, 118, 125, 136, 141; pole,
    131, 136, 141; runner, 125
beautyberry, 59, 125
beavers, mountain, 184
beer, for slugs, 169–70
bees, 178: bees, leafcutter, 171; bees,
    mason, 178
beetles, 130, 131; controls, 173, 175;
    cucumber, 175; flea, 136, 153,
    176–77; ground, 169, 175; ladybug,
    173; soldier, 178; striped cucumber,
    175; western spotted cucumber, 175
beets, 131, 136, 141, 177
beneficial insects, 178
Berberis, 125
bergenia, 124, 125, **plate 25**
big leaf maples, 188
bindweed, 144, 145, **154**; field, 154;
    hedge, 154
bird houses, 115
birds, 169
bishops weed, 190
bittercress, little western, 144, 154, **155**
black spot, 119, 159, 164–65, 187–88
black widow spider. *See* spider
blackberries, 125; diseases of, 161;
    evergreen, 150; Himalayan, 145,
    150
Blechnum spicant, 121
blight, early, 135, 163
blight, late, 135, 163
Bloedel Reserve, WA, 192
blood grass, Japanese, 79, **plate 6**
boomers. *See* beavers, mountain
borage, 118, 125, 142
boron, 50
botrytis, 135
box elder, 161
box elder bugs, 168, 170
boxwood, 78, 117, **plate 1**
bricks, 69, 131

British Columbia, Canada, 91, 102,
    144
British gardens, 109
broccoli, 136; flea beetles in, 177
broom 'Vancouver Gold', 85
brunnera, 90, 112, 124
Brussels sprouts, 132, 136
buddleia, 101, 188, 189
buddleja. *See* buddleia
bulbs, 94
bush beans. *See* beans, bush
Butterfield Cottage Garden, OR, 195
butterflies, 101, 174
butterfly bush, 101, 143. *See also*
    buddleia
butterfly houses,115
Buxus, 117, **plate 1**

cabbage, 131, 136, 141, 142, 161
cabbage, Chinese, 132; flea beetles in,
    177
cabbage moths, 131
calcium, 134
calendula, 107, 189
California, state of, 102, 144
California ground squirrel. *See*
    squirrel
California lilac, 102
California wax myrtle, **121**, 122, 194
calla lilies, 189, **plate 32**
Callicarpa bodiniere 'Profusion', 59,
    125
Calluna spp., 123
camellias, 99, **100**; diseases of, 166
campanula, 125
Canadian thistle, 149–50
candytuft, 117
canker, 157; bark, 166
canna lilies, 93
Cardamine oligosperma, 154–55, **155**
Carex macrocephala, 79, **81**
Carex obnupta, 79, **80**
carpenter ants, 168
carrots, 131, 136, 141, 142; carrot flies,
    131
caterpillars, 174

Daphne odora, 59, 86
Darmera pelatum, 107
daylilies, 104,124
deadhead, 99; of herbs, 118
deciduous plants, 2, 3, 51, 59, 85, 104, 121, 123, 124; azaleas, 64, 98, **99**
deer, 94, 95, 180, 183–84
deer fern, 121
delphinium, 125
deodara cedar, 101
design, 55
determinate tomatoes. *See* tomatoes
diagnosing diseases, 158
dicentra, 125
dill, 131, 141
dinosaur food plant, 87
diseases, 156; bacterial, 157; black spot, 119, 159, 164–65, 187–88; cycles, 157, 160; diagnosing, 158; environment for, 132, 157; host plants, 132, 157; immune, 159; infectious, 156; non-infectious, 156; pathogens, 132, 156–57; powdery mildew, 119, 139, 157, 164–65, 187; resistance, 130, 159; rust, 159; signs, 158; symptoms, 158; vegetables, 131, 32; viral, 156–57
disinfecting wipes, for tools, 60
doublefile viburnum, 59
Douglas fir, 123
Douglas squirrel. *See* squirrel
dragonflies, 178–79
drip irrigation, 51, 68, 90, 135, 160; for vegetables, 128
drought, 51
drought-resistant gardening, 90, 92
dry gardens, 74
Dryopteris ferns, 122; *D. erthrosora*, **plate 24**; *D. filix-mas cristata*, **123**
Dublin, Ireland, 109
Dudleya farinosa, 81
dune gardening, 67, 80, 112, 117, 121; cottage-style dune gardening, 120–24
dusty miller, 124
dwarf coyote bush, 85

early blight, 135, 163
Eastern red cedar, 84
echinacea, 93, **94**, 125
Edinburgh, 109
eggplant, 118, 132, 188; flea beetles in 177; diseases of, 161
elderberry, red, 123
elevation, 1, 2, 89, 90, 92
elk, 94, 180, 183; Roosevelt elk, 183
Elymus mollis, 78, **79**
England, 109
English cottage gardens, 55, 109–110
English holly, 59
English ivy, 143, 145, 146, **147**, 188, 189. *See also* weeds
English laurel, 86
entomology, 168
environment, disease in, 132, 157
Epilobium angustifolium, 155
Epilobium ciliatum, 156
Equisetum arvense, 148, **149**
eradication, 158
Erica, 123, **plate 24**
Erigeron glaucus, 80
Erysimum menziesii, 80
escallonia, **85**, 117
euonymous, 125, **plate 1**
euphorbia, 93, 105, 125; *Euphorbia characias wulfenii*, **87**; *E. esula*, 153; *E. peplus*, 153
European beach grass, 78, 145
European cranberry bush, 59
European cranefly, 172
evergreen blackberry, 150
evergreen honeysuckle, 103
exclusion of disease, 158

fall interest, 58–59, 64
feather reed grass, 124
fences, 3, 52, **53**, **115**, 117
fennel, 118, 125
ferns, 51, 57, 121–22, 124, 125, **plate 24**; native, 121
fertilizing, Mediterannean, 97
fertilizing, vegetables, 129, 130
fescue. *See Festuca glauca*

lilacs, problems with, 161, 170
lilies: deer and elk, 180; thrips in, 174.
    See also *Hemerocallis* (daylilies)
lily, turf, 117
lime, 134, 139
liriope, 117
lithodora, 106
little western bittercress, 144, 154, **155**
loam soil, 49, 50, 101
location, 53–54, 128, 159
London, 109
Lonicera, 104, 105, 117
loosestrife, 143, 144
lopping shears. *See* shears
loupe, 168
lupines, 80, 116, 124; *Lupinus*
    arboreus, 80

madrone, Pacific, 52, 121, **122**
magnesium, 50
mahonia, 125
Mahonia aquifolium, 122–3
maidenhair ferns, 121
maidenhair tree, 58
maintenance, 56, 74, 83, 111; in
    vegetable gardens, 130
mallow, 125, **plate 27**
manzanita, 52, 93, 194
maple trees: big leaf, 188; diseases in,
    161; Japanese, 77, 125, 188, **plate 4**,
    plate 5; vine, 58, 188
marigolds, 130, 142–42, 189
mason bees, 178
McNeilan, Jan, 4
McNeilan, Ray, 4
Meditation garden, 74, 75, 78, 82, 83,
    116, **plate 3**
Mediterranean bulbs, 94
Mediterranean colors, 92
Mediterranean gardens, 90, **91**, **plate**
    10, plate 11
melons, 132
Menzies' wallflower, 80
metaldehyde, 169
Mexican orange, 125
Miami River, OR, 100

mice, house, 180, 181
microclimates, 3, 4–5
mildew, powdery, 119, 125, 139, 157,
    159, 164
Mingus Park, Garden, OR, 193, **plate 3**
mints, 68, 125, 131, 142, 190
mixed borders, 117
moles, 143, 172, 180, 182; coast, 182
mollusks, 168
monarda, 107, 125, 142
monkshood, 103
mosquitoes, 176
moths, 174, 175; cabbage, 131
Mount Hood, 72
mountain beavers. *See* beavers,
    mountain
mountain gardening, 89
mugho pine, 84
Muhlenbergia capillaris, 87
mulch, 59, 94, 97, 104, 105, 111, 119,
    146, 183; tomatoes, 135
muscari, 94
Myrica californica, **121**, 122

Nandina domestica, 59
nasturtium, 124, 125, 131, 141–42
native plants, 52, 72, 78, 95, 116, 117,
    120, 144, 148, 171, 180; native
    ferns, 121; native grasses, 116
nematodes, 130–31, 157
nepeta, 125
New Zealand flax, **75**, **124**
Nitobe Memorial Garden, BC, 191
nitrogen, 50, 167
non-infectious diseases, 156
North American dune grass, 78
northern sea oat grass, 124
Northwest Mosquito and Vector
    Control Association, 176
Norway rats. *See* rats
Norway spruce, 123
noxious weeds, 101, 144, 148, 152
nurseries, 55, 62, 63, 64, 78, 99, 160

oat grass, northern sea, 124
obelisks, 115

beetles in, 177; sweet potatoes, 132, 184

potential problems, 143

pots, 55, 59, 60, 78, 82, 92, 93, 112, 117, 118, 169, 189, 190

potting sheds, 59–60

powdery dudleya, 81

powdery mildew, 139, 157, 159, 164, 165, 187

preserving tools, 61

preying mantis, 178

princess flower shrub, 118, **plate 23**

problems, 143

Prunus laurocerasus, **86**

Prunus x subhirtella, 125

Pseudotsuga menziesii, 123

pumpkins, 139, 141; pumpkins, diseases of, 161

purple cone flower. *See Echinacea*

purple loosestrife, 143, 144

purple sage, 125

purslane, 87

pussy willow, 123

Queen Anne's lace, 145

Quercus garryana, 95

Quercus ilex, 84

Quinault River, WA, 100

raccoons, 184–185

radishes, 125, 131, 139, 141, 142

ragweed, 145

rain, acidity of, 116

rainfall, 3, 4, 5, 50, 51, 90, 162

raised beds, 52, 57, 67–70, **68, 69, 70,** 84, 89, 128, 129, 134, 163; materials for, 68–71

ranunculus, 94

raspberries, 125; diseases of, 161, 162, 163

rats, 180; Norway, 180; roof, 181

recycling plants, 117

red alder, 101

red elderberry, 123

red hot poker, 106

red-twigged dogwood, 59, 124

redbud, 161

reed grass, 124

rhododendron, 98, 99, 105, 107, 116, 123, **plate 1, plate 13**; diseases of, 166; rhododendron bug, 175–76; *Rhododendron mollis,* **99**

rhubarb, 139

riparian areas, 100, 101, 107, 125, 126, 144, 150, 186, 199

rivers, 100

rockroses, 92

rocks, 69, 74–75, 83, 131

rodent proofing, 181

roof rats. *See* rats

Roosevelt elk. *See* elk

root rot, 158, 162

root weevils, 170

Rosa rugosa, 120, 125, 143, 144

rosemary, 92, 95, 117, 118, 125, 131, 180

roses, 50, 51, 54, 57, 90, 105, 113, 117, 119–20; aphids, 167, 173; black spot, 159, 164; climbing, 119, 125; diseases of, 161, 164–5; fertilizing, 119; fungal diseases, 119, 159, 164; fungicides, 119, 164; hybrid tea, 119, 187; leafcutter bees in, 171; petal count, 119; powdery mildew on, 157, 159, 164; pruning, 119–20; rust on, 159; salt winds, 119; shrub, 117, 125; systemic foods, 119, 164; wind, 119

rotation, crop, 71, 131–32, 135, 157, 158, 162, 163

row covers, 134–35, 136, 139, 175, 177

Rubus laciniatus, 150; *R. procerus,* 150

rudbeckia, 93, **95, plate 11**

Rumex acetosella, 153

rushes, 124, 125

Russian sage. *See* sage, Russian

rust, disease, 125, 136, 159, 165

rust, on tools, 61

rusty willow, sawfly in, 172

sage, 125, 131; purple, 125; Russian, 102

salal, 52, 116, 117, 121, 123, 125, 144

viburnum, 86, 125, 161; *Viburnum opulus*, 59; *V. plicatum tomentosum*, 59

Vinca major, 190

vine maples, 58, 188

vine weevils, on yew, 102

viral organisms, 156–57

virticillium wilt, 161

virus, hosta, 165–66

viruses, 156–57

voles, 183

walls, 68, 69, 92, 98, 106, 111, 113, 115, 128,

Washington, state of, 4, 51, 54, 79, 80, 89, 91, 100, 144, 168, 172, 183, 189, 199

Washington Park Arboretum, WA, 192

wasps, parasitic, 173, 175, 178

water, 48, 51, 52, 56, 64, 74–75, 77, 82, 90, 92, 102

water molds, 162–63

watering, 63, 72, 93, 96, 97, 98, 129, 135, 160

wax myrtle, California, **121**, 122

weather vanes, 53

webs: insect, 158; spider, 179

weeder tools, 60

weeds, 143; annual, 145; in vegetable garden, 130; noxious, 144; perennial, 145; seeds, 145

weevils, root, 170

weigela, 125

well-drained soil, 55, 94

western red cedar. *See* cedar

western spotted cucumber beetle, 175

western willow, sawfly in, 172

whistlers. *See* beavers. mountain

whiteflies, 177–78

willow, coral embers, 124

willow herb, purple leaved, 156

Wilson River, OR, 100

wilting, 158, 162, 170

wind, 1, 2, 3, 4, 5, 48, 52, 53, 54, 83, 84, 113; wind breaks, 3, 84; windscreen, **53**, 115, 117

Winter daphne, 59, 86

winter interest, 59, 88, 95, 98–99

winter squash, 133, 140

wisteria, 124

witch hazel, 59, 125

woodsorrel, creeping red, **151**

xeriscape, 90, **91**, 95–97, 98; plants for, 97, 98, 101, 102, 107

xylem, 163

yarrow, 52, 98, 103, 124

yaupon, 85

yellow flag iris. *See* iris

yellow garden spider. *See* spider

yellow sand verbena, 80, **plate** 7

yellow star thistle, 144, 152

yellow-striped armyworm, 174

yellow-twigged dogwood, 59, **96**

yew, 102, 117

yucca, 118

Zen gardens, 55, 57

zinnias, 107

zones, USDA, 3, 4, 90

zones, AHS, 3, 4

zucchini, 140

ABOUT THE AUTHOR

Carla Albright is an Oregon State Master Gardener as well as a Penn State Master Gardener who writes a gardening column for the *Tillamook Headlight Herald*. She teaches OSU Master Gardener classes and works as a professional gardener in several coastal gardens in Oregon. Albright's floral and landscape photos have been published in several Pennsylvania magazines.

www.ingramcontent.com/pod-product-compliance
Lightning Source LLC
Chambersburg PA
CBHW082102030125
19757CB00002B/7

9 781589 793170